D1449093

Margaret J. Barr, *Northwestern University*
EDITOR-IN-CHIEF

M. Lee Upcraft, *The Pennsylvania State University*
ASSOCIATE EDITOR

Contributing to Learning: The Role of Student Affairs

Steven C. Ender
Indiana University of Pennsylvania

Fred B. Newton
Kansas State University

Richard B. Caple
University of Missouri–Columbia

EDITORS

Number 75, Fall 1996

JOSSEY-BASS PUBLISHERS
San Francisco

CONTRIBUTING TO LEARNING: THE ROLE OF STUDENT AFFAIRS
Steven C. Ender, Fred B. Newton, Richard B. Caple (eds.)
New Directions for Student Services, no. 75
Margaret J. Barr, Editor-in-Chief
M. Lee Upcraft, Associate Editor

© 1996 by Jossey-Bass Inc., Publishers. All rights reserved.

No part of this issue may be reproduced in any form—except for a brief
quotation (not to exceed 500 words) in a review or professional work—
without permission in writing from the publishers.

Microfilm copies of issues and articles are available in 16mm and 35mm,
as well as microfiche in 105mm, through University Microfilms Inc., 300
North Zeeb Road, Ann Arbor, Michigan 48106-1346.

ISSN 0164-7970   ISBN 0-7879-9931-8

NEW DIRECTIONS FOR STUDENT SERVICES is part of The Jossey-Bass Higher
and Adult Education Series and is published quarterly by Jossey-Bass Inc.,
Publishers, 350 Sansome Street, San Francisco, California 94104-1342.
Periodicals postage paid at San Francisco, California, and at additional
mailing offices. POSTMASTER: Send address changes to New Directions for
Student Services, Jossey-Bass Inc., Publishers, 350 Sansome Street, San
Francisco, California 94104-1342.

SUBSCRIPTIONS cost $52.00 for individuals and $79.00 for institutions,
agencies, and libraries.

EDITORIAL CORRESPONDENCE should be sent to the Editor-in-Chief,
Margaret J. Barr, 633 Clark Street, 2-219, Evanston, Illinois 60208-1103.

Cover photograph by Wernher Krutein/PHOTOVAULT © 1990.

Manufactured in the United States of America on Lyons Falls
Pathfinder Tradebook. This paper is acid-free and 100 percent
totally chlorine-free.

CONTENTS

EDITORS' NOTES

During the past two decades, there has been a visible demand by the public for higher education to demonstrate its value with concrete educational outcomes, and higher education is responding in a variety of ways. College student affairs, as an integral part of higher education, is working to help formulate this response and demonstrate its contribution to achieve appropriate learning outcomes for students. Although student affairs continues to function from a foundation of essential student services, the profession is showing evidence of achieving new levels of educational activity. For at least twenty-five years, student affairs has been offering student development programming; now there is evidence of increased effort to enhance the campus learning environment with emphasis on both affective and cognitive learning experiences.

We believe the profession of college student affairs has always been concerned with student learning but has been too prone to let others determine the nature of that learning, who is responsible for its occurrence, and how it can be better achieved. There is evidence that a discussion of the proper role for college student affairs in this all-important enterprise is growing and that the result may be a new level of activity for the profession of college student affairs. It is our hope that what is presented here will contribute in a positive way to the nature of this discussion.

This sourcebook has as its primary purpose the investigation and reporting of the present realities of the student affairs profession regarding mission, purpose, and impact on student learning. In Chapter One, we present the results of a national survey of chief student affairs officers that focused on three philosophical models that guide the profession and the extent to which campus programming is devoted to each. Additionally, findings regarding programming practices related to learning, the enhancement of learning, and the overall learning environment are discussed. The results of the survey indicate that student affairs is heavily invested in the learning process.

Chapter One supports the proposition that student affairs is devoting considerable resources to the enhancement of student learning, and the next six chapters describe a number of ways in which these resources are employed. These chapters discuss learning propositions, the role of the student affairs learning consultant, student affairs professional expectations, and programming practices that stimulate, support, and enhance student learning and the learning environment. In all the chapters, theory is translated to practice by illustrations of exemplary programs presently being implemented across the country.

In Chapter Two, Fred Newton and Joanne Smith review some of the recent literature on how students learn, identifying several factors that make a difference in the learning process. Specific learning propositions that can be translated into student affairs practice are shared, with discussion of their usefulness throughout higher education.

In Chapter Three, Richard Caple discusses a relatively new role for the student affairs professional—that of learning consultant. Specific areas of consultation are discussed, including assessment and research, student peer groups, conflict resolution, student activity transcripts, and learning disability programs.

Kenneth Ender, Sunil Chand, and Jerry Sue Thornton present in Chapter Four the particular challenges facing the student affairs professional in the community college setting. Specific expectations of a student affairs division dedicated to the enhancement of student learning are presented. These expectations apply across the landscape of student affairs regardless of type of institution.

Chapter Five discusses the unique contributions of new student orientation in regard to student learning. In this chapter, Debra Robinson, Carl Burns, and Kevin Gaw present implications for student learning through orientation programming related to transition issues, academic adjustment, and personal and social integration.

Garry Johnson and Kathryn Cavins provide a review of the literature related to residential life and its impact on student learning in Chapter Six. The chapter provides a clear rationale for the importance of residential living and its positive effects on learning outcomes.

In Chapter Seven, John Schuh provides a description of the various academic courses offered by student affairs professionals. Common features of these courses are presented as well as expected learning outcomes. Some speculation regarding the future of courses taught by student affairs is shared.

In Chapter Eight, under the leadership of Richard Caple, we conclude the sourcebook with our explanation of where the field of student affairs is potentially heading in respect to the profession's contribution to the student learning mission of higher education.

Throughout the sourcebook, we have attempted to provide the reader with as many examples of exemplary practice as space would permit. As we began the sourcebook we solicited examples of learning enhancement programs. This request yielded 270 program descriptions from across the country. Information on how to contact institutions whose programs were mentioned or described in this sourcebook can be found in the Resources section at the back.

Finally, a word of thanks to Michelle J. Donohue, a master's candidate in the IUP Student Affairs in Higher Education program, and Cindy Ferringer, an undergraduate mathematics major at IUP. Donohue served as a graduate intern to the editors and was particularly helpful in reading and sorting the program descriptions submitted for this volume. Ferringer served as a research assistant to the editors and conducted much of the data analysis presented in Chapter One. As educators, we are always amazed by the competence of our students and are grateful for their willingness to teach us!

Steven C. Ender
Fred B. Newton
Richard B. Caple
Editors

STEVEN C. ENDER *is professor in the Learning Center, Division of Student Affairs, Indiana University of Pennsylvania.*

FRED B. NEWTON *is director of counseling and professor of counseling and educational psychology at Kansas State University.*

RICHARD B. CAPLE *is director of counseling and professor of education at the University of Missouri–Columbia.*

Student affairs contributes daily to student learning, academic success, and the learning environment.

Contributions to Learning: Present Realities

Steven C. Ender, Fred B. Newton, Richard B. Caple

Striking changes are occurring across the landscape of higher education and there is little doubt that student personnel professionals, departments, and entire divisions are and will continue to be part of this change. As Guskin (1994) observes, "Colleges and universities today face their most significant crisis in over 40 years . . . the analysis of this crisis has coalesced over the last year with a focus on the double-edged sword of costs: the expenses of institutions are too high for their revenues and the costs of what we offer are growing beyond students' (and their families') capability or willingness to pay" (p. 23). Compounding the fiscal challenges facing higher education, the academy is also confronted with a resounding and recurring call from students, families, and other important constituents—including state legislatures, accreditation boards, and the public in general—to increase campus opportunities for student learning and to demonstrate learning outcomes.

It seems obvious that it will become increasingly important for all campus educators, including those in student affairs, to demonstrate their contribution to the learning process and subsequent learning outcomes that occur on campus.

Friction over Dwindling Resources

There is little doubt that restructuring, reengineering, and downsizing are the dominant words presently facing higher education. Guskin (1994) reported that at least 50 percent of the public universities have experienced midyear budget cuts for each of the past two years. A number of major universities have had no salary increases for two to three years. These budgetary concerns have led to competition for scarce dollars between the faculty and student affairs professionals. As Wagener and Lazerson (1995) note:

> Staff members in student services argue that students have become their responsibility by the default of the faculty . . . faculty members, insisting that they are the university, do not want budgets for student support to remain large or to continue growing . . . at issue is the breakdown of a complex bargain, negotiated at the end of the 1960s: The expanding psychological, academic, and career-counseling needs of students would be met by personnel in either student services . . . or academic services. . . . Faculty members would be released from primary responsibility for counseling students, provided that professors conducted research. College and university administrators implemented that bargain by providing resources for both research and student support. [p. 60]

University administrators can no longer afford to pay for that bargain and it seems clear that student affairs, its programs, and personnel must be able to clearly demonstrate ongoing and significant contributions to student learning and student academic success if the profession is to continue to develop beyond its basic service function. As Ward (1995) observes, "Students come to our campuses to learn, and we must improve our ability to deliver the goods to them. . . . Student affairs must begin to play a larger, more visible role in engaging students in the learning process and, by extension, enhancing institutional productivity. . . . If we do not completely engage students in the learning process we will become irrelevant" (p. 14).

Response from Student Affairs

As debate and discussion occur nationally regarding measures to curtail the rising costs of higher education while simultaneously delivering expanding learning opportunities to students, there is another and related discussion occurring within the profession of student affairs. That discussion involves the issue of purpose. More specifically, is there a primary raison d'être for student affairs on the college campus?

The Learning Imperative. Student affairs, as represented through professional leadership in the American College Personnel Association, recognized a need for the profession and its membership to demonstrate renewed professional vitality on college campuses. The need to transcend the role of service providers and promote a rationale for programs and services that are developmental and learning oriented in nature as part of the profession's mission was recognized. This recognition was clearly demonstrated through formulation and publication of *The Student Learning Imperative: Implications for Student Affairs* (American College Personnel Association, 1994). This publication, which indicated its purpose was to stimulate discussion regarding how student affairs professionals can intentionally create campus conditions that enhance student learning and personal development, highlighted the considerable discussion taking place within the profession about this issue.

Presently, in professional associations, journals, and annual, regional, and state conferences, one can hear the ongoing and at times intense rhetoric of professional philosophy and purpose. Clearly, lines are being drawn and age-old debates are resurfacing. As a profession, are we service providers, developmental educators, or professionals primarily committed to promoting student learning and academic success?

This debate is clearly articulated in publications such as *Reform in Student Affairs: A Critique of Student Development* (Bloland, Stamatakos, and Rogers, 1994), a monograph that severely questions the choice of student development theory as the predominant model of student affairs work. Instead, it argues for the past roots of the profession as service providers and facilitators of student learning and academic success. The visceral response of Brown in "Reform in Student Affairs: A Counterpoint Comment" (1995) provides clear evidence of the sharp differences of opinions and professional orientation of some of the leading thinkers and scholars in the student affairs profession. He states, "This monograph is not what it purports to be: a scholarly and analytical critique of student development . . . instead, it is a misinterpretation and misrepresentation of what student development theory, philosophy, research, and practice is about (p. 12)."

A Response to the Debate. As the debate continues, as most recently presented through a recent special issue of the *Journal of College Student Development* titled "The Student Learning Imperative" (Schroeder, 1996), there seems to be a need for better answers to questions that transcend the debate and focus instead on present professional realities, questions that address the profession and help clarify its present practices and future directions. These include What are the predominant philosophical models and modes of thinking that presently guide student affairs leadership? What is the relative importance of student services, student development, and student learning as constructs for practice? How do divisions of student affairs improve student learning and the academic success of students? Where do learning opportunities for students emerge within student affairs organizations? What percentage of student affairs resources are devoted to student learning, student development, and student service? Do practitioners evaluate their programs for effectiveness and measure the learning outcomes they purport to instill in students?

Survey

To answer these and other questions regarding present student affairs practices on today's campuses, the authors implemented a national survey. This project, discussed in detail in "Student Affairs: Philosophical Models and Program Initiatives" (Ender, Newton, and Caple, 1996), was designed in part to assess the importance of the primary philosophical models in student affairs and the extent to which these models define campus practice and provide direction for resource allocation. The extent to which campus programming reflected the intent of the models was also assessed, as was the extent to which practitioners believe the models should guide professional preparation programs in student affairs. The research, conducted over the summer and fall of 1995, consisted of a survey questionnaire developed by the authors and mailed to 560 chief student affairs officers (CSAOs) selected at random from the National Association of Student Personnel Administrators (NASPA) mailing list. This list consisted of the 1,125 voting delegates to NASPA. An initial mailing of the survey and two follow-ups generated a 76 percent response rate or 430 completed and returned questionnaires.

Models. The CSAOs were asked to rate the importance (on a scale of 1 to 10, 1 being most important and 10 least important) of three philosophical models as these models guided the work and resources of their divisions. They were also asked to rate the extent to which they believed the models should provide direction to student affairs graduate preparation programs. The three models were student services, student development, and student learning. Definitions for each model were provided by the survey authors.

Student Services Model. Under this model, the primary purpose of student services is to support the academic mission of the institution by providing the numerous adjunctive services (admissions, housing, counseling, student activities, recreation, financial aid, and so on) that are necessary to maintain the student in the classroom. Philosophically, this model promotes learning outside the classroom, sometimes referred to as extracurricular, and seeks to meet the basic needs of students as they matriculate.

Student Development Model. This model represents the maturation process that human beings go through from birth to death. College student affairs professionals guided by this model focus on the developmental phases or tasks that students experience as they pursue a college education. Many different theories are used in this model and have been categorized as person-environment interaction, psychosocial, cognitive-development, and topological theories. The developmental concepts embedded in this model represent the philosophical criteria for making decisions about implementing student affairs programming on campus.

Student Learning Model. The student learning model places its emphasis on shared efforts with other educators, faculty, and administrators to achieve a more integrated or seamless learning experience. The emphasis is on establishing learning goals or outcomes and assessing the success that is achieved. Outcomes of this model are primarily related to intentional learning, academic assistance, and enhanced academic climate. Learning is broadly defined to include content knowledge in both cognitive and affective areas.

Within the survey instructions, respondents were reminded that each of the models have similarities and draw their definitions from overlapping literature. Model differences lie in their perceived role, emphasis, and implementation. Additionally, it was acknowledged that most student affairs divisions and programs would, in all likelihood, sponsor programs that originate from all three models or orientations, but the survey sought to determine, among other outcomes, the relative importance of each model in guiding day-to-day student affairs work.

Results. Table 1.1 presents the results of the 430 respondents. These results are sorted demographically, indicating the importance of each model to guide professional practice, preparation programs, and campus resource utilization. First, the relative importance of each model to guide professional practice is represented by a mean score (SSM = student services model, SDM = student development model, and SLM = student learning model). Second, the relative importance of each model for guiding graduate preparation programs (GSSM = graduate student services model, GSDM = graduate student development model, and GSLM = graduate student learning model) was determined by computing a mean score for each model. Finally, to determine how resources were employed in divisions of student affairs, CSAOs were asked to determine the percentage of division time and energy that is devoted to each model. A mean percentage of time (%SS = percentage of time student services, %SD = percentage of time student development, and %SL = percentage of time student learning) was calculated for each model.

Philosophies Guiding Campus Practices. A review of Table 1.1 demonstrates that student affairs chief executives as a group are first guided by the constructs represented by the student services model, followed by student development and then student learning. All three models are deemed as important as demonstrated by the low mean scores generated for each. When we analyzed the data to determine which model was rated as most important, 50 percent (*n* = 213) chose student services, 20 percent (*n* = 87) chose student development, 16 percent (*n* = 67) chose student learning and 13 percent (*n* = 55) chose more than one model, the mixed model, as equally important.

The allocation of resources as represented by the percentage of time and division effort devoted to the constructs of each model reinforces the importance of student services when guiding professional practice. Again, for the entire group, student services occupies half the time and energy of professionals in practice (51 percent), followed by student development (28 percent) and student learning (21 percent).

In most instances, there seems to be remarkable consistency between the model chosen as most important by the respondents and the amount of division time and effort devoted to each of the three models. The highest percentage of time and effort devoted to student services (60 percent) is reflected by those 213 respondents who also identified student services as their philosophical model of first choice. The same is true for the 87 respondents who identified student development as their first choice. That is, they also devoted the largest percentage of division time and effort to student development activities. Even though the 67 who chose student learning first did not devote their highest percentage of division time and effort to student learning activities, they did devote more resources to this area (28 percent) than any other demographic category that we analyzed.

We are not surprised to discover the philosophy of student services leading the way in campus practice. Services as reported in the survey are the core

Table 1.1. Demographic Responses by Model Type

	SSM	SDM	SLM	GSSM	GSDM	GSLM	%SS	%SD	%SL
All (n = 430)	3.27	3.89	4.43	3.61	3.50	3.70	51%	28%	21%
M1 (n = 213)	1.71	4.51	5.06	2.75	3.52	3.60	60	23	17
M2 (n = 87)	4.47	1.90	4.49	4.11	2.41	3.77	38	39	22
M3 (n = 67)	5.60	4.69	2.37	5.37	4.41	3.12	43	30	28
M4 (n = 55)	4.61	3.67	4.40	4.14	4.14	4.69	46	29	24
2 year (n = 55)	2.82	3.90	4.60	2.71	3.10	3.63	58	26	16
4 year (n = 375)	3.34	3.90	4.40	3.73	3.56	3.71	50	28	22
Public (n = 223)	3.22	3.87	4.43	3.45	3.43	3.70	53	27	20
Private (n = 98)	3.37	3.94	4.34	3.80	3.61	3.62	48	30	22
Doctoral (n = 102)	3.15	3.43	3.89	3.61	3.13	3.31	50	29	21
Master's (n = 127)	3.77	4.38	4.63	3.95	3.97	4.04	50	27	23
Bachelor's (n = 139)	3.16	3.82	4.60	3.67	3.50	3.71	49	30	21
Associate (n = 55)	2.82	3.90	4.60	2.71	3.10	3.63	58	26	16
Less than 3,000 (n = 177)	3.27	4.10	4.49	3.67	3.50	3.75	51	28	21
3,000–10,000 (n = 132)	3.13	3.85	4.55	3.37	3.48	3.57	53	27	21
10,000–20,000 (n = 71)	3.42	3.41	4.00	3.58	3.32	3.40	47	31	21
More than 20,000 (n = 45)	3.60	4.00	4.27	4.02	3.76	4.38	53	26	21

Note: SSM = mean score, student services model, SDM = mean score, student development model, SLM = mean score, student learning model. GSSM = mean score, graduate student services model, GSDM = mean score, graduate student development model, GSLM = mean score, graduate student learning model. %SS = percentage of time student services, %SD = percentage of time student development, %SL = percentage of time student learning.

of our profession and will continue to be so for the foreseeable future. We are, however, somewhat surprised to discover the importance of the student learning philosophy to CSAOs, considering the relatively recent focus on this construct as a major emphasis in student affairs. It seems clear that CSAOs are paying attention to the national debate, devoting more than 20 percent of division time to programs addressing the constructs of this area. We do not know if this represents a change from past practice. However, in a related survey question, 75 percent of the respondents indicated that their student affairs division is expected to devote even more time and energy in the future to support student learning and student academic pursuits.

Professional Preparation Programs. The respondents again rated all three philosophies as important in guiding the content of professional preparation programs. Student development was the most important (M = 3.50), followed by student services (M = 3.61) and then student learning (M = 3.70). The means are so close it would seem that all three are about equal in importance. This is different from the practice side, where student services clearly was rated as more important than the other two models. Again, it is interesting to note the relative importance of student learning as compared to the other two more recognized philosophies in the field of student affairs.

Philosophical Models: Our Conclusions. One objective of this survey was to provide some concrete information regarding the contributions of student affairs to learning and to seek some answer to the ongoing discussion of purpose. The issue of professional direction is important to the profession. However, the ability of student affairs to prove itself in the ever-increasing battle for campus resources is essential. We believe these results demonstrate that the concept of student learning as a philosophical model to guide our professional practice in student affairs is viable. A full one-third (33 percent) of the survey respondents could identify an official campus entity (commission, committee, and so on) that brought together educators from both student and academic affairs for the purpose of supporting student learning.

Considering the relatively recent focus within the profession on student learning, these results are surprising. Although student services remains the bread-and-butter work of student affairs on most campuses, it is encouraging to note the substantial place of student development (with 28 percent) and student learning (with 21 percent) of division time and energy devoted to programmatic focus. To devote 21 percent of student affairs resources and time to issues of intentional learning, academic assistance, and enhancement of the academic climate may seem to some far too little, but it seems to the authors an encouraging sign. We believe this finding illustrates the importance CSAOs are placing on the national concern about educational outcomes in the face of the reality of limited resources and changing priorities.

Learning Opportunities in Student Affairs

Survey respondents were asked, "Of all the departments and agencies in Student Affairs, which one spends the most staff time enhancing student learning on campus?" Six departments stood out as principal contributors to student learning and were mentioned by substantial numbers of respondents. These included: residence life (26 percent), counseling (25 percent), learning enhancement programs (24 percent), student life (23 percent), career planning (11 percent), and student development (4 percent).

Residence Life. Chapter Five presents a thorough review of the importance of residence life as it affects student learning on campus. Survey data that support the importance of residence life include 69 percent of the respondents responsible for residence life on their campuses said programs that stress academics were offered in their halls, 36 percent sponsored special academic floors as a housing option, and 15 percent said that faculty members were living in the halls.

Counseling. Survey data that support the importance of counseling center activities as they relate to student learning include: 80 percent of the respondents said their division sponsored study skills workshops—many offered by counseling center staff. Also, 24 percent said they assessed the learning styles of students and 36 percent assessed the academic readiness levels of entering students. Sixty-two percent of the respondents said their divisions sponsored formal courses that taught helping skills to student paraprofessionals and 73 percent sponsored programs that explicitly assist students in the area of values clarification. Many of these programs were sponsored by counseling center staff.

Learning Enhancement Programs. Learning center type programs are well represented in student affairs. Of the survey respondents, 43 percent said they sponsored a learning center or its equivalent in their division. Fifty-three percent said they offered a tutorial program. Also, 71 percent said their division either offered or participated in a campuswide early warning system to identify freshmen experiencing academic difficulty. Of the 92 percent of the respondents who said their institution offered a program to assist students with learning disabilities, 61 percent of these programs were located in student affairs. Formal study skills courses were offered by 14 percent of the respondents' divisions. Remedial math was offered in 6 percent of the divisions, followed by remedial English (5 percent) and remedial reading (3 percent).

Student Life. In the survey, 97 percent of the respondents had an office of student activities in their division. In this area, interesting findings associated with student learning include: 72 percent sponsored programs that focused on the arts, theater, and other events targeting the aesthetic development of students; 71 percent offered a lecture series that brought one or more major external speakers to campus each semester; and 87 percent sponsored programs that focused on enhancing race relations. Also, 81 percent sponsored or participated in academic experiences designed to reinforce service learning and community service opportunities and 9 percent of the respondents offered formal, credit-bearing courses associated with service and community learning.

Student affairs is heavily involved in offering student leadership development as a learning opportunity for students. Of the respondents, 95 percent said their division sponsored programs in leadership development and 18 percent offered formal courses in leadership development.

In view of the educational advantages to deferred rush (Terenzini, Pascarella, and Blimling, 1996), it is encouraging to see that 47 percent of the respondents who sponsored Greek life programs required those programs to practice deferred rush practices and 65 percent of the Greek life programs practiced a policy of maintaining minimum acceptable cumulative grade point averages to be recognized by the institution.

Career Planning. Eighty-four percent of the respondents had departments of career services within their divisions and 11 percent identified this office as the primary contributor to student learning on campus. Career planning courses were offered by 24 percent of the institutions surveyed. Survey respondents mentioned the value of cooperatives and internships as well as résumé writing, interviewing skills, and life planning as important learning activities offered through offices of career planning.

Student Development. Many opportunities for student learning are available through student development programs. Although only 23 percent of our survey respondents offered a program or center for student development as an official agency or department, 26 percent had a staff member titled *director of student development, student development specialist,* or *coordinator of student development* and 39 percent said their division offered formal opportunities for students to assess their personal development and establish goals and objectives to master developmental tasks. Of these, however, only 5 percent required students to participate in these formal types of developmental learning opportunities.

Measuring Learning Outcomes

Although student affairs is achieving broader input into the learning process on college campuses and offering many types of programs that promote student learning, personal development, and academic success, the profession continues to have problems evaluating these programs. Specifically, 66 percent of the survey respondents said that they systematically produce data that evaluate and support the effectiveness of the programs sponsored by their division. Stated in another way, it seems that three out of ten programs are not producing data to guide, support, and justify their programs and the campus resources that are necessary to offer them.

Nationally, higher education is experiencing significant pressure to produce outcome data that measure student learning. Accreditation agencies such as Middle States have recently mandated colleges and universities to demonstrate outcome assessment plans as part of the ten-year institutional review. Clearly, institutions are being challenged to demonstrate what students learn, how well are they learning it, and how the institution knows they are learning it (Middle States Association of Colleges and Schools, 1991).

The survey demonstrates that there is still some distance to go in regard to measuring learning outcomes, however. According to the results of the data

Why not try to get in with existing ones

analysis, 25 percent of the divisions surveyed have adopted and implemented a formal outcomes assessment program. Of the 75 percent that have not developed such a program, 59 percent say they are in the process of developing one. These results are worthy of professional consideration. As we continue into the foreseeable future in a climate of fiscal austerity and public distrust regarding the use of resources and the measurement of outcomes, failure to have learning outcomes data available could signal the weakening of the profession over the years to come. Long gone are the days where program justification could be based on the numbers of students that show up or the positive way they evaluate their experience. We must be able to demonstrate that our programs are resulting in significant learning experiences for students—that is, learning experiences and outcomes that are valued by the academy and the general public.

Summary of Findings and Implications for the Future

The following statements summarize the most significant results of our national survey. Possible implications of these results for professional consideration are offered.

• The overall survey response rate (76 percent) coupled with the CSAOs' requests for survey results (86 percent) indicates their extremely high interest in examining present professional philosophies that guide student affairs practice and preparation programs and the implications of those philosophies in regard to campus-based student affairs–sponsored programs. *Implication:* Student affairs, as a profession of individuals, is at a point of restating and perhaps redefining its role and function in American higher education. Whereas *The Student Learning Imperative: Implications for Student Affairs* (American College Personnel Association, 1994) and *An American Imperative* (Wingspread Group on Higher Education, 1993) provided examples of professional organization interest in this issue, the results of our survey underline the significant impact and interest of this movement on the practice level.

• The student services model prevails as the predominant functional purpose for student affairs today. However, the student development model and the student learning model seem to be gaining a place as additions to student affairs campus purpose and practice. One can view these additions much like new rooms being added to an old house. As the two newer functions are added the old still needs to be maintained. *Implication:* Divisions of student affairs are accumulating campus responsibilities. Although this may have evolved out of history and necessity, now may be the time for student affairs programs to review organizational structure and functions to determine the need for reorganization, prioritization of responsibilities, and redirection of resources. On today's campuses, strategic planning and reengineering are two current examples of this process. It is to be hoped that student affairs will not find itself left out of what many may perceive as an academic process and focus.

- Student affairs launches learning-oriented programs primarily through five departments or agencies: housing, counseling, learning centers, student life, and career services. Staff from these offices have become the main campus providers in the implementation of programs designed to enhance learning functions, such as study skills laboratories, learning disability assistance, orientation, service learning, and adviser training. Over 75 percent of the CSAOs responding to the survey perceive that the demand for staff time and energy devoted to learning enhancement programs will increase in the immediate future. *Implication:* Certain student offices are more likely to be involved in learning programs than others. This may be due to such factors as the relatedness of the learning functions to the offices' traditional functions, staff initiatives, and the staff's preparedness for carrying out these programs. As more and more learning enhancement programs evolve from student affairs departments, there is a need to find ways to have flexible staffing patterns that will link units and develop coherent programs that serve students in a systemwide, coordinated manner. Greater effort should be made to complement the academic affairs division and academic departments to provide an academic program that will appear consistent to students.

- CSAOs believe that professionals should receive training in areas represented by the student learning model at levels of importance equal to training in student development and service functions. *Implications:* To fully prepare professional staff with expertise in student learning, staff training must include the knowledge base and skill training appropriate for working in these areas. The theoretical basis of training should be carefully reviewed and determined. Professional training might include knowledge in theory areas such as learning, motivation, personality and learning style(s), social psychology, and student development. Preservice and inservice training, as now provided, may not be sufficient to provide these qualifications and may need to be supplemented or enhanced.

- Twenty-five percent of CSAOs report the presence of an outcomes assessment program within their division. Of the rest, 59 percent indicate that they are working toward including outcomes assessment as part of the staff's responsibility, emphasizing the need for accountability data to demonstrate linkage of program effort to student academic success. *Implication:* Student affairs staff must establish outcome-based accountability for demonstrating program impact on student success. Outcome standards, appropriate modes of measurement, and accountability reports will serve to inform all members of the academic community of the efficacy of student affairs program efforts. *not necessarily*

- In an effort to offer exemplary practical examples of learning enhancement programs sponsored by divisions of student affairs, the authors solicited and received descriptions of over 270 programs for review. *Implication:* Professional staff are presently involved in both the development and implementation of programs that enhance student learning. Many are innovative and creative, and involve collaborative efforts with colleagues from academic affairs.

The profession may benefit from a sharing of these ideas through the use of clearinghouses, on-campus sections of professional journals, workshops, and presentations at national, regional, and state conferences.

• Our data indicate that 75 percent of student affairs programs presently report through the CSAO to the president of the university. This means that one out of four programs are reporting to someone other than their institution's chief decision maker. The survey identified that about half of those not reporting to the president reported to an administrator in academic affairs and the others in areas of enrollment management. Also, of those now reporting to the president, 5 percent indicated that the organizational structure of their institution was changing and they were soon to be shifted to a reporting line different from the one now enjoyed with the president. *Implication:* Even though most student affairs divisions now report to the president, three out of ten find themselves in the organizational position of not having the attention of the institution's chief executive officer on a day-to-day basis. Student affairs personnel, through attention to learning and outcomes assessment, can work to justify their legitimacy to faculty, students, and institutional administrators— thereby ensuring that student affairs will continue to be a significant stakeholder on college and university campuses for years to come.

Some Final Thoughts

The winds of change are swirling through most college and university campuses. This chapter has provided a glimpse of that change as viewed by chief student affairs officers providing leadership at 430 institutions of higher education. Clearly, these high-ranking administrators have a significant voice in the manner in which policies are developed to guide campus practices. They are in significant positions to allocate resources to manage current challenges and institutional priorities. It is clear to us that these individuals value the impact student affairs is making and will make in the future in regard to how students learn, what students learn, and the environment in which learning takes place. Student affairs is a significant stakeholder in the educational mission of higher education. As a profession it has responded successfully to all past calls for changes in higher education that have a direct bearing on students. It is our belief that the profession will successfully respond to this new call for accountability with increased contributions to student learning.

References

American College Personnel Association. *The Student Learning Imperative: Implications for Student Affairs.* Washington, D.C.: American College Personnel Association, 1994.
Bloland, P. A., Stamatakos, L. C., and Rogers, R. R. *Reform in Student Affairs: A Critique of Student Development.* Greensboro, N.C.: Erie Counseling and Student Services Clearinghouse, 1994.
Brown, R. D. "Reform in Student Affairs: A Counterpoint Comment." *ACPA Developments,* 1995, 22 (4), 12.

Ender, S. C., Newton, F. B., and Caple, R. "Student Affairs: Philosophical Models and Program Initiatives, A National Survey of Chief Student Affairs Officers." *A Report to Survey Respondents.* Indiana, Pa.: Indiana University of Pennsylvania, 1996.

Guskin, A. E. "Reducing Student Costs and Enhancing Student Learning." *Change,* July/Aug. 1994, pp. 23–29.

Middle States Association of Colleges and Schools. "Teamwork for Outcomes Assessment." Commission on Higher Education, Nov. 1991, pp. 1–41.

Schroeder, C. C. (ed.). "The Learning Imperative." *Journal of College Student Development,* 1996, 37 (2), 113–253.

Terenzini, P., Pascarella, E., and Blimling, G. "Students' Out-of-Class Experiences and Their Influence on Learning and Cognitive Development: A Literature Review." *Journal of College Student Development,* 1996, 37 (2), 149–162.

Wagener, U. W., and Lazerson, M. "The Faculty's Role in Fostering Student Learning." [Point of View.] *Chronicle of Higher Education,* Oct. 1995, p. A60.

Ward, L. "The Student Learning Imperative: From Innovation to Implementation." *ACPA Developments,* 1995, 22 (2), 14.

Wingspread Group on Higher Education. *An American Imperative: Higher Expectations for Higher Education.* Racine, Wis.: Wingspread Group on Higher Education, Johnson Foundation, 1993.

STEVEN C. ENDER is professor in the Learning Center, Division of Student Affairs, at Indiana University of Pennsylvania.

FRED B. NEWTON is director of counseling and professor of education at Kansas State University.

RICHARD B. CAPLE is director of counseling and professor of counseling and educational psychology at the University of Missouri–Columbia.

This chapter provides a summary of key propositions on how college students may optimize their learning experience through programs and interventions offered by those in student affairs positions.

Principles and Strategies for Enhancing Student Learning

Fred B. Newton, Joanne H. Smith

Student affairs professionals are being asked to demonstrate their contribution to student learning and to aggressively form partnerships with faculty to help students attain positive learning outcomes. Our goal in this chapter is to organize what is known about the learning process as propositions that can guide student affairs professionals toward the design and implementation of strategies that enhance academic success.

There are several questions that need to be addressed if we are to understand the process of student learning and determine ways that the process of learning may be facilitated. How do students learn best? What needs to be done to enhance a learning environment? How do all facets of the educational community collaborate toward selected institutional goals? These are questions facing all personnel of a campus community. Student affairs professionals must now define their unique and important contribution in this process.

Dimensions of Student Learning

Crucial to the development of successful intervention programs designed to facilitate student learning is an understanding of how students learn. It is possible to identify a set of attitudes, behaviors, and skills that foster the acquisition of learning. However, the process requires us to address the question of what is meant by the term *learning*. Barr and Tagg (1995) make clear the distinction between learning and teaching. Teaching or instruction is a method and not an end of education. When the emphasis is placed on the outcome of learning, the rewards of an educational system support a variety of processes, which may include—but are not limited to—teaching.

Michael (1975) identifies seven cognitive competencies and skills that represent general intellectual outcomes of college. They include individual ability to process and apply new information; to communicate effectively; to reason objectively and draw conclusions from various types of data; to evaluate new ideas and techniques efficiently; to become more objective about beliefs, attitudes, and values; to evaluate arguments and claims critically; and to make reasonable decisions in the face of imperfect information.

Angelo (1991) organizes learning around four dimensions that may vary as a focus in a classroom or educational environment. Student affairs professionals can work with faculty to determine which dimensions fit best to a variety of classroom experiences as well as programs and activities of students occurring outside the classroom setting.

Dimension 1: Declarative learning in higher education is learning the facts and principles of a given field. It is learning the "what" or content of the discipline. Students are commonly assessed by how well they have learned relevant facts and principles by asking them to declare their knowledge in speech or writing. Most college curricula are aimed to promote gains in this dimension of learning.

Dimension 2: Procedural learning describes how students learn to do things by acquisition of the processes and procedures involved. There are very specific skills that college students are expected to master. For instance, most faculty are interested in helping students improve their skills in critical thinking, public speaking, and clarity of writing. There are also specific skills particular to each specialty that need to be mastered if one is to be considered proficient in the discipline. The mix of general and specific skills taught in college makes up the procedural dimension of learning.

Dimension 3: Conditional learning is understanding when and where to apply knowledge and skills one has mastered. The student must apply good judgment in the particular field. Conditional learning is knowing the time and situation in which knowledge can be applied for the greatest advantage. Case study methods, clinical instruction, and one-to-one coaching are methods used to train and reinforce this dimension.

Dimension 4: Reflective learning in higher education is a focus to help students become independent lifelong learners. Students learn ways to reflect on their own interests, motivations, attitudes, and values. By learning to be self-reflective and individually initiating, they understand why they believe, think, and act as they do in a value-consistent manner.

Mission statements of nearly every institution of higher education are reflective of each institution's interpretation of educational purpose and learning outcome. Angelo (1993) defines *higher learning* as an active, interactive process that results in meaningful, long-lasting changes in knowledge, understanding, behavior, dispositions, appreciation, and belief (p. 4). Learning is more than cognitive development; it includes social and emotional aspects as well.

How do students learn? Basic principles of student learning have been described in the literature. Angelo (1993) discusses thirteen research-based principles that can guide efforts to maximize learning. Strange (1994) describes fourteen propositions, variables that consider both individual and environmental impact, of how development occurs with college students. Still others have shown how specific principles can be directly implemented through intervention programs. Examples of these include Halstead's (1993) sixteen principles for improving academic performance and Newton's (1990) six dimensions of impact for underachieving students. Astin (1993), Pascarella and Terenzini (1991), Pascarella and others (1996), and Tinto (1993) are among those who have summarized research on how student learning is affected by the college experience. This research leads to summary propositions regarding how students learn.

Student Learning: Propositions for Making a Difference

Learning is best facilitated when it is ends-directed. Campbell used the comment, "If you don't know where you're going, you'll probably end up somewhere else," as the title of a book (1974). This title could easily reflect on the importance for a learner to be focused so as to know and act with intention toward personal goals. Students are motivated by understanding the purpose of what they are doing and by being aware of the connections between the educational content of course work and their daily activity and personal aspirations. Angelo (1993) indicates that it is important for goals to be explicit, reasonable, positive, and congruent in a way that fits with the goals of the educator.

On the other hand, we know that many students come to college expressing confusion, uncertainty, and indecision about who they are, what they want, and where they are going in life. For these not atypical students, a reasonable initial goal in the academic environment is to gain awareness of personal interests, knowledge, and abilities, and to explore a range of possible experience. A compatible educational environment would provide opportunities for self-awareness and personal exploration through orientation experiences, career counseling, broad-based curricular offerings, mentoring, internships, and similar advising activities. As students develop clarity of goals they will need the opportunity for planning, articulating, and transferring academic goals to life aspirations.

Learning is optimal when the student's level of engagement reflects a commitment to educational activity. Astin (1993) found that involvement was the overriding variable of importance in the determination of student academic success. Pascarella and Terenzini (1991) describe involvement as engagement or as a volitional commitment to occupy one's attention and behavior toward educational goals. Angelo (1993) indicates that active learning is preferred to passive learning. Active learning occurs when students invest physical and mental energy in activities that make their learning meaningful. Active learning requires attention and focus rather than detachment, indifference, or aloofness. Factors that determine level of engagement are temporal, spatial, and psychological. The quantitative and qualitative amount of time spent in educational activity is a major determining factor in student success. Similarly, physical presence in an environment that supports or maintains learning activity influences the educational attainment. Students who live and work on campus, who interact with faculty outside as well as in the classroom, and who organize and manage their time will increase their chances to have positive educational outcomes.

While all of these conditions may be necessary, the student must additionally have sufficient motivation to be personally invested in the activity. For example, in a study of high-risk students, it was found that merely providing the opportunity and the activity to improve a student's learning process has little impact on certain students who refuse to invest significant time and energy in the task (Hamlin, 1986). A responsibility of student affairs professionals is to understand how to challenge and stimulate the motivation of students.

Learning is affected by individual difference in style, developmental level, perceptions, and background experience. Strange (1994) overviews how students differ in the rates at which they resolve developmental tasks. Because of these differences, there are various points of readiness that will influence the learning moment for a student. He also points out that students differ in how they have constructed a worldview, individual impressions for perceiving reality that will cause some students to think and act differently from others in the same environment. Variation may occur as a result of diversity from ethnicity, gender, or other distinguishing background features.

Research has also shown that people vary in personality and learning style, resulting in differences in preference for approaching and acting on a situation. For example, using the Myers-Briggs typology of personality style, it has been found that students often have difficulty interacting in a classroom with a professor who operates from a different personality type. In many cases, the student may have a preference for structure and detail, a sensing/judging type, and becomes lost or confused with open-ended assignments by an instructor who prefers to look at the big picture and allow the students multiple options, an intuitive/perceiving type (Schroeder, 1993). The congruence of a learning experience to a preferred personal style will affect the student's comfort and understanding of an academic situation.

Student affairs professionals potentially have the training to assess, understand, and intervene in ways that consider individual differences. Expertise in developmental theory, learning style, perception, and cultural difference can be an asset when student affairs staff serve as consultants in the planning and designing of educational interventions to meet these differences.

Student approaches to learning tasks become habituated patterns of responding and acting. A major contribution of behavioral psychology is the description of how people form habituated responses to certain situations. For example, we know that learning often takes place in small incremental steps (typically, one learns to crawl and then to walk). Practice and consistency are factors in the formation of response patterns to familiar conditions. Habits once learned become difficult to unlearn and change. Often students learn to study in inefficient and self-defeating ways that lead to poor performance. They may have learned wrong or they may have gotten by with ineffective behaviors in less complex or less difficult learning situations. The difficult yet necessary choice for many of these students is to change these study habits or face failure. Feedback processes may provide outcome data that help the students make adjustments and improvements in effective responding. The task of forming sufficient patterns of study must include feedback on study results and may include the unlearning of ineffective habits and the subsequent learning of effective methods.

Other principles of learning refer to how students connect data and make associations. For example, from gestalt psychology, we know that people tend to organize data in ways that are meaningful and capable of being remembered. Effective methods of recognizing and organizing data will affect the way a student reads, outlines a text, takes notes, or even memorizes a list of ideas. Using the analogy of the brain as a computer, the task becomes one of developing adequate software to access the capacity of the memory potential in an efficient manner.

There are many implications of these principles that can be used to promote student learning. Halstead (1993) has outlined a program for college students in academic difficulty that puts to practical use sixteen learning principles for students who have unproductive learning habits. It has been our experience that low-achieving students need to incorporate methods of gaining feedback on what they did wrong on a test or a paper so they can make corrections for future preparation. Corrective strategies include the comparison of their own study behavior with an ideal standard and the identification of what would need to be done to achieve improvements. When change of study behavior is indicated, an emphasis is then placed on support strategies to reinforce the change and overcome previous ineffective habits. Students working in a support group follow through with commitments to take action and achieve specific goals they have identified. Data were collected over a six-year period with students going through this type of program. They were tracked on measures of grade point average, retention in the program, and completion of degree. These students demonstrated dramatic improvements over matched counterparts not in the program (Newton, 1990).

Student affairs practitioners must recognize that interventions designed to improve study methods require more than a content class on how to study. Such interventions must incorporate knowledge of human development, personal preference, and learning acquisition as part of the process.

Learning is influenced by self-concept and sense of personal efficacy. The beliefs one has about oneself can be a major determinant of whether a person will act in a successful manner. Individuals make personal self-appraisals of how well they will execute actions to deal with prospective situations. Bandura (1982) describes this behavior as self-efficacy. He indicates that people attain a sense of self-efficacy through past experiences, observance of other people's successful behavior, reassurance and verbal encouragement from others, and a confident recognition of adjustment ability to new situations (Bandura, 1982). Research supports the relationship between self-efficacy and academic performance (Multon, Brown, and Lent, 1991).

Covey (1989) describes how effectively functioning people focus their energy on the areas of life in which they can recognize a sense of personal influence. By maintaining focus on the areas of influence they avoid getting caught up in futile and time-consuming activity in which they have no control. People with a sense of self-efficacy believe they can exert effort with good results, that they will solve problems when encountered, and can make adjustments to new situations. Those without this sense will often see their actions as futile, may tend to blame the external environment for their difficulties, and can become despondent and listless about their situation.

It is important for professionals in a learning environment to assess a student's self-concept and encounter each student in a way that can positively affect the student's perception of how to achieve academic success. For example, the authors have noted many low-achieving students who describe themselves as "dumb" and refer to remedial classes as "bonehead" math or English. Interventions that will modify and change these impressions are essential to enhance the probability of success. To strengthen self-efficacy, students must observe a model of successful behavior that they can emulate. They must succeed in some initial ways to gain confidence, and they must recognize how success in one arena can transfer to another.

For example, an adult student who was quite successful as a night manager in a restaurant was struggling in his economics class. An adviser provocatively remarked to the student that he seemed to know how to handle his business, and suggested he view the class as a business, and so approach classroom requirements in a similar fashion. The student reflected on the parallels and came back the next day with an outline of how his business strategies— such as using expert consultation, time and task organization, and team effort—could apply to the class. Also, for the first time, the student expressed enthusiasm in approaching this class. Similarly, a student athlete experiencing great success on the playing field labeled himself a "dumb jock" sitting in the back of the classroom. However, when challenged by the instructor to be the "team captain" of a group project in which the entire group would be evaluated for a presentation, his attention immediately picked up and he worked twice as hard as his peers to assure that his group would not fall behind.

The maintenance and improvement of one's overall well-being can affect the successful accomplishment of learning goals. Lloyd-Jones (1954) was one of the first to emphasize the importance for student affairs workers of attending to the whole person. A well-rounded student pays attention to physical, social, spiritual, and psychological needs. Kobasa (1979) found that "hardy" people manage stressful events and make successful adjustments in life where others might falter and become victims of stress or illness. Stress due to a variety of pressures is the most common set of symptoms reported by students seeking assistance at college counseling centers today (Murray, 1996). The ability to manage stress and stressor events can affect a student's immediate ability to cope with a critical situation and maintain academic progress. It also can become a life management skill that extends beyond the college experience and lays the groundwork for a healthy, happy, more satisfying lifestyle.

Many campuses are now providing wellness programs incorporating both assessment and education for leading a healthy, well-balanced life. These programs may derive from a variety of student affairs professionals including health educators, counselors, recreation leaders, and residence hall staff. Programs include topics on physical fitness, nutrition, social support, stress management, and personal problem solving. The University of Wisconsin–Stevens Point has established a model for the implementation of a campuswide wellness program. Student affairs practitioners may provide the link to consider the holistic dimensions of personal well-being and assist the students in learning the skills and attitudes for self-regulation of mind and body.

The social and environmental milieu will affect individual learning for better or for worse. People exist in a system in which there is constant exchange of energy between the boundaries of the individual and the environment. These contact points may support, stimulate, nourish, and challenge the individual to extend personal boundaries and enhance potential. On the other hand, these contact points may be threatening and intimidating to the individual's perceived integrity and cause withdrawal and reduce exchanges with the outside forces. Systems theory suggests that the reduction of energy exchange and contact will allow entropy to proceed—or in the case of the learner, lead to a deterioration of the potential to grow (Caple, 1985). It is important for the practitioner to be aware of the way the interaction system will affect educational goals.

The contact environment may be described in several ways. Strange (1991) categorizes four descriptive models of the human environment. The *physical model* addresses the bricks and mortar, the facilities, the equipment, the aesthetic setting, and other physical resources of the institution in which the student exists. The *human aggregate model* reflects the collective characteristics of the environmental milieu as set by the people inhabiting the space. These could include the norms, social customs, ethnic identification, reputation, and other sociological factors. The *organizational model* focuses on how the structure and the purpose of the institution will impose parameters on a situation. Organizational examples include how the institution identifies priorities, rewards faculty accomplishment, or sets standards and codes of conduct. The *perceptual model* describes the subjective personal impression an individual experiences in an environment that may be based as much upon expectations, past experience, and anticipation as upon the external reality.

Each of these aspects of an environment may influence the performance of individual students. Individuals will have a sense of themselves in the environment that can be reflected by factors such as fit or compatibility, comfort level, amount of challenge and stimulation, contact with faculty, and even the potential to receive personal recognition. The human aggregate impression may be reflected by the external reputation and status of the campus, and internally, on campus, by measures of community noted through a sense of belonging, collegiality, and support. The organization may measure its consistency and integrity toward stated institutional purpose by the manner in which its structure and procedures work toward these goals. Finally, the physical resources may be noteworthy quantitatively by the number of volumes in the library or the size of the football stadium and qualitatively by unique or exceptional facilities and equipment.

Interventions to intentionally shape the environment are best accomplished by systemwide efforts. Kuh (1996) has described this principle as a "seamless" educational environment. It is probably too idealistic to hope that a campus that values academic freedom, individual faculty prerogatives, and tolerance of diverse opinions can also provide a seamless experience. However, it is very important for the major players who shape the educational environment to come together and agree on the priorities and purpose of the institution and its milieu. This calls for cooperative and coordinated strategies across all facets of the campus. Some institutions have moved toward strategic planning, reengineering, and transformation processes that address broad-based methods for implementing change and direction at an institution level. However, it is also noted that every campus can be broken down into smaller units that are the main identification points for students. The development of living units as environments with specific outcomes such as self-governance floors, quiet atmosphere, and mentoring relationships are but a few examples that have implications for student affairs staff.

Example Programs and Interventions

Many exemplary programs are being implemented by student affairs practitioners in all types of college and university settings around the country. The national survey of chief student affairs administrators (CSAOs) reported in Chapter One indicates that the four student affairs offices responsible for the greatest numbers of these programs are residence life, counseling, learning centers, and student life. However, it is less important to note the departmental origin of academic assistance programs than to know the when, where, and how of the intervention. For this reason, the following examples are given by categories: preparation and adjustment of new students, assessment and diagnosis of student learning, learning assistance intervention programs, and impact of intentional living and learning environments.

Preparation and Adjustment of New Students. Tinto (1993) indicates that effective orientation programs go beyond the provision of information per se to the establishment of early contacts for new students not only with members of their entering class but also with other students, faculty, staff, and campus resources. Mentor programs typically employ faculty, staff, or upper division students to serve as informal advisers and campus shepherds to guide new students through the period of separation and transition to the life of the college. Variations of mentor programs can be found at California State University at Fullerton, the University of New Mexico, Colorado State University, Notre Dame College of Ohio, North Seattle Community College, and Southwest Texas State University. Texas Tech University has a program called PRIDE (Peers for Retention, Interaction and Diversity in Education) that helps new and transfer minority students deal with cultural and personal adjustment and study skill concerns as they begin their academic experience.

A number of institutions offer continuing orientation credit classes, often as cooperative efforts between academic colleges and student affairs staff. These classes, known around the country as *University 101* (Gardner and Jewler, 1985), orient, overview, and introduce new students to campus life through topics such as personal adjustment, study habits, and learning styles. Activities in these classes may range from the very practical—how to locate campus resources—to discussion and exploration of personal and social issues confronting students such as dating, relating to roommates, and alcohol consumption. The Academic Assistance Center at Kansas State University provides topical overview lecture sessions taught by staff from a variety of offices across campus and then conducts small-group discussion seminars run by trained peer assistance leaders. The Counseling Center staff at the University of Missouri–Rolla provide a resource handbook to support faculty advising and provide training through faculty development seminars. At the University of Kentucky, counselors provide Teaching and Learning Effectiveness Workshops for faculty demonstrating how the student's personality style is affected by the structure and methods of learning used in the classroom. Counseling staff at the University of Louisville offer "guest appearance" lectures on Skills for Success topics to faculty who may have reason to need their classes covered on a given day. Chapter Five provides a more in-depth description of orientation programs.

Assessment and Diagnosis of Student Learning. Early warning systems have been developed on many campuses to intervene with students having learning difficulty before it is too late. A decision must be made at each institution whether to be intrusive or just hope that students will seek assistance when they need it. Some institutions have decided that the former course is a necessary strategy. Preenrollment assessments are often used to identify high-risk students and intervention begins at that point. Indeed, the federally funded Upward Bound program was founded on the principle that preparation before entrance to college would increase the opportunity for success. Cooperative ventures between academic and student affairs offices have been made to identify early indications of grade difficulty. Prompt and timely feedback and response by those that can assist students is an essential element in the effectiveness of these systems to retain students.

At Walla Walla Community College and the University of Wisconsin–Oshkosh, early warning begins during the fourth week of class and is initiated by faculty in their classrooms. They use faculty-developed monitoring forms to note the incidence of classroom behaviors typically associated with academic difficulty. Students and support staff who offer assistance programs are notified at that point to initiate intervention.

For other institutions, confrontation of students in academic difficulty occurs the first semester they go on academic probation. Academic success support groups that run from five weeks to the entire semester have been implemented to provide probationary students an opportunity to adopt successful study behaviors. Success programs have been implemented at Eastern Montana College, Worcester Polytechnic Institute, and Kansas State University. The University of Illinois provides a similar program using individual contact with a student paraprofessional. This program, called AIM, provides support, identification of problem areas, and problem solving for probation students who choose to participate.

Accurate assessment of why and where students go wrong academically is a resource now being developed on many campuses. The Learning Enhancement Assessment Program (LEAP) was developed by staff at the Counseling Service of Kansas State University as literally a "weigh station" and "distribution center" for students identified by faculty and student affairs staff as having academic difficulty. The *weigh* aspect includes an assessment of several individual dimensions affecting student performance, including learning style and methods, motivation and direction, anxiety and affective reactivity, and self-concept. The *distribution* function helps the student in locating resources on or off campus that can provide appropriate assistance.

Learning Assistance Centers. According to the CSAO national survey, a learning assistance center or similarly titled office exists at over 40 percent of the surveyed campuses. These centers generally offer learning support resources to improve academic skills through individual or group tutoring, supplemental instruction seminars, and skill development programs in areas such as reading textbooks, taking notes, managing time, and preparing for tests. At Southwest Texas State University this program is made accessible to students by providing tutors, workshops, and classes in places like residence halls and the library. Student affairs staff also reach out to work directly with faculty in the classroom and campus clubs or organizations through presentations and workshops on topics such as learning strategies, effective self-management techniques, and how to make positive changes in academic habits. Some programs have put together printed materials that are distributed or made easily accessible to students as a self-help resource. Examples include a series of eight learning improvement tip sheets developed by the Counselling Service at University of Waterloo and fifteen Help Yourself brochures written and distributed by staff of the Counseling Service at Kansas State University.

Impact Through Living and Learning Environments. Many programs have been designed to help students increase responsibility for their own learning by increasing interaction with faculty out of the classroom, and by making the social and living environments supportive of academic outcomes. The

Gradevine program at Southwest Texas University is an example. A computer-generated report is distributed to each residence hall providing residents with a cross index of other students in their hall who are enrolled in the same courses. This allows the opportunity for students to make contact for study and test review sessions. Residence staff and faculty are also invited to participate in residence hall programming based upon identified needs.

Thiel College (Pennsylvania) offers the Dead Lecture Society, where faculty get involved through lecture-discussions in residence halls on stimulating and often nontraditional topics such as creative dating or racism. The University of Nebraska–Lincoln has a program called Residence Life Faculty Fellows, which targets undergraduates who are interested in interacting with faculty and student affairs professionals. Sixteen teams, each including a faculty member and someone from student affairs, meet periodically on a residence hall floor in discussion groups.

Integrating and collaborating learning programs with residence halls have been carried out in a variety of forms including Learning Clusters (LaGuardia Community College), Federated Learning Communities (Western Washington College, Centralia College), and Residential Colleges (Yale, Stanford, University of Maryland, Michigan State University). First-year programs have combined orientation and residence life programming with the intent of helping new students integrate intellectual and social life (University of Washington).

Other programs have linked student social and cultural life to academically relevant themes. The School of Preparatory Studies at Gallaudet University has worked with the Student Life Office to integrate student activities with what students are studying in the classroom. Before each semester begins, there is a meeting with the chairs of several departments to look at course syllabi so that the student life staff can plan activities around the academic schedules developed by faculty. Faculty may then require students to attend a program or give extra credit for their participation. Faculty report that students typically contribute more to class discussions after attending a student life program.

The greater the cooperation among the many offices of academic affairs and student affairs, the higher the potential for a congruent and supportive learning environment exists throughout the institutional community. Akron University has a campuswide committee composed of faculty and student affairs staff to study the learning climate of its university community. Similarly, Valparaiso University (Indiana) has a Student Learning Task Force committed to an interdisciplinary initiation of learning in the total university system.

Epilogue

The program examples described in this chapter illustrate how student affairs practitioners are engaged in a vast array of interventions that promote student attainment of learning goals. The national survey of CSAOs reported in Chapter One indicates that the vast majority of student affairs staff are involved from point of recruitment and orientation until graduation. Involvement includes student advising and planning, classroom instruction, diagnostic assessment of learning styles and problems, faculty development, enhancement of learning atmosphere in living environments, interventions with social groups, and accommodation and support of those with special learning needs. Another promising aspect of many of these programs is evidence that they are producing outcomes data to measure their impact.

These programs hold promise for the contributions that student affairs staff can make toward student learning goals, but there are still concerns and limits for what is being accomplished. Three important needs must be addressed by student affairs.

Coherent Learning Program Efforts. Although most of the CSAOs surveyed said they valued student learning activities as an important function of student affairs staff, they also estimated that only about 20 percent of staff time is directly related to learning programs. A majority of this activity was attributed to four offices (residence life, counseling, learning centers, and student life). Student affairs divisions are predominantly structured around the student services model with activities that follow the traditional functional tasks, thereby leaving individual offices to determine how they will develop and organize learning programs. Today, the impetus for program development may result more from individual or agency initiative than through coherent divisionwide attempts to achieve broad learning enhancement goals. Strategic planning or similar goal-setting methods are needed in which organizations develop specific and institutionally consistent objectives to better focus efforts toward divisionwide student learning goals.

Articulation with Academics. One problem that may exist on many campuses is the separate organization and perceived difference in mission between student affairs and academic affairs. As noted in the example section of this chapter, some cooperative programs uniting student affairs offices with academic colleges or departments have demonstrated positive student success outcomes. A criticism of unfocused effort has pointed to waste and redundancy where services are duplicated across many offices. A by-product of redundancy is the unnecessary confusion students may have about where to find the appropriate service.

In still other cases, different parts of an institution may send conflicting or contradictory messages to students. For example, one academic department may take a sink-or-swim attitude to their freshman students, enrolling them in tough classes where only the fittest survive, while another department in the same college provides orientation classes and identifies potential at-risk students for special interventions to improve retention rates. Another example is a situation where an alcohol education program publicizes the advantage for academic success of responsible levels of drinking while a Greek organization promotes "a drink till you drown" party. Coordination and consistency of the priorities on campus is a prerequisite for a institution to seek an intentional learning environment. The first step on campus is providing a campuswide forum to determine these priorities. A positive note from the CSAO survey was the response that nearly one-third of the institutions could identify a coordinating group such as a committee, task force, or centrally responsible office that served to coordinate a collaborative student learning agenda.

Outcome Accountability. Value-added and other consumer-oriented expectations have confronted institutions with the need to be more responsive in demonstrating the impact of classes, curricula, services, and programs on student success. Demonstrating impact can be a difficult, time-consuming activity, but it is necessary to meet the challenge of the future. Research and data collection to identify student needs and measure the impact of intervention are initial steps. Even more important is the challenge of understanding the complex matrix of variables that impinge upon and affect student learning. Methods of qualitative research can assist the practitioner and the learner to understand the nuances and the complexity of individual differences and consider the impact of the social context. Some student affairs offices have developed annual reports that read like stockholders' statements, summarizing the impact of services through both summative outcome data and more in-depth case examples that illustrate for students, faculty, and staff how student learning can be affected by the programs of the office.

Today, student affairs professionals are at the threshold of possibility to become main players in a process where higher education will focus on the breadth and depth of student learning. Examples of student affairs contributions are many and varied, and the challenge is to demonstrate a coherent, integrated approach made in concert with the academic community and with clear and measurable outcomes.

References

Angelo, T. A. (ed.). *Classroom Research: Early Lessons from Success.* New Directions for Teaching and Learning, no. 46. San Francisco: Jossey-Bass, 1991.

Angelo, T. A. "A Teacher's Dozen: Fourteen General Findings from Research That Can Reform Classroom Teaching and Assessment and Improve Learning." *American Association of Higher Education Bulletin,* Apr. 1993, pp. 3–8.

Astin, A. W. *What Matters in College? Four Critical Years Revisited.* San Francisco: Jossey-Bass, 1993.

Bandura, A. "Self-Efficacy Mechanism in Human Agency." *American Psychologist,* 1982, *37* (2), 122–147.

Barr, R. B., and Tagg, J. "From Teaching to Learning: A New Paradigm for Undergraduate Education." *Change,* Nov./Dec. 1995, pp. 13–25.

Campbell, D. *If You Don't Know Where You're Going, You'll Probably End Up Somewhere Else.* Niles, Ill.: Argus Communication, 1974.

Caple, R. B. "Counseling and the Self-Organization Paradigm." *Journal of Counseling and Development,* 1985, *64* (3), 173–178.

Covey, S. R. *The Seven Habits of Highly Effective People.* New York: Simon & Schuster, 1989.

Gardner, J. N., and Jewler, A. J. *College Is Only the Beginning.* Belmont, Calif.: Wadsworth, 1985.

Halstead, R. W. *The 16 Principles: A Guide to Getting Better Grades in College.* Worcester, Mass.: COB Press, 1993.

Hamlin, J. "The Effect of a Self-Management Method on Retention and Academic Performance of Marginal Students." Unpublished doctoral dissertation, College of Education, Kansas State University, 1986.

Kobasa, S. "Stressful Life Events, Personality, and Health: An Inquiry into Hardiness." *Journal of Personality and Social Psychology,* 1979, 37 (1), 1–11.

Kuh, G. D. "Guiding Principles for Creating Seamless Learning Environments for Undergraduates." *Journal of College Student Development,* 1996, 37 (2), 135–148.

Lloyd-Jones, E. "Changing Concepts of Student Personnel Work." In E. Lloyd-Jones and M. R. Smith (eds.), *Student Personnel Work as Deeper Teaching.* New York: HarperCollins, 1954.

Michael, R. "Education and Consumption." In F. Juster (ed.), *Education, Income, and Human Behavior.* New York: McGraw-Hill, 1975.

Multon, K. D., Brown, S. D., and Lent, R. W. "Relation of Self-Efficacy Beliefs to Academic Outcomes: A Meta-Analytic Investigation." *Journal of Counseling Psychology,* 1991, 38 (1), 30–38.

Murray, B. "College Youth Haunted by Increased Pressure." *APA Monitor,* 1996, 26 (4), 47.

Newton, F. B. "Academic Support Seminars: A Program to Assist Students Experiencing Academic Difficulty." *Journal of College Student Development,* 1990, 31 (2), 183–186.

Pascarella, E. T., and Terenzini, P. T. *How College Affects Students: Findings and Insights from Twenty Years of Research.* San Francisco: Jossey-Bass, 1991.

Pascarella, E. T., Whitt, E. J., Nova, A., Edison, M., Hagedorn, L. S., and Terenzini, P. T. "What Have We Learned from the First Year of the National Study of Student Learning?" *Journal of College Student Development,* 1996, 37 (2), 174–181.

Schroeder, C. C. "New Students—New Learning Styles." *Change,* Sept./Oct. 1993, pp. 21–26.

Strange, C. "Managing College Environments: Theory and Practice." In T. K. Miller, R. B. Winston, Jr., and Associates, *Administration and Leadership in Student Affairs.* (2nd ed.) Muncie, Ind.: Accelerated Development, 1991.

Strange, C. "Student Development: The Evolution and Status of an Essential Idea." *Journal of College Student Development,* 1994, 35 (6), 399–410.

Tinto, V. *Leaving College: Rethinking the Causes and Cures of Student Attrition.* (2nd ed.) Chicago: University of Chicago Press, 1993.

FRED B. NEWTON *is director of the Kansas State University Counseling Services and professor of counseling and educational psychology.*

JOANNE H. SMITH *is director of residence life at Southwest Texas State University, San Marcos, Texas.*

A rationale for student affairs professionals to serve as campus consultants on student learning is presented. Particular areas in which they can work with students and faculty as consultants are identified, and examples are provided.

Student Affairs Professionals as Learning Consultants

Richard B. Caple

In the beginning, American colleges provided an integrated learning environment in which students lived together and went to class under the supervision of the same mentors. As the nation grew, institutions of higher learning grew in size too, and knowledge expanded at a rapid rate until it became necessary to divide the task of governing each college. Student affairs was created to help manage the growing colleges and universities. But from the beginning, student affairs professionals were cast in a supporting role to the main actors in the classroom and functioned almost entirely outside the formal classroom. In time, faculty became increasingly specialized, discipline-centered, and were rewarded less and less for good teaching or work with students outside the classroom. The result was a dualism in institutions of higher learning viewed as in-class and out-of-class activity in which students could easily become lost.

Lloyd-Jones and Smith (1954) pointed out the dualistic nature of higher education with its emphasis on mind and body, reason and emotion that was applied in the classroom and in extra-class activity, "teaching by faculty on one hand and counseling by student personnel workers on the other" (p. 11). It was, Lloyd-Jones suggested, not unlike the medical model of treatment in which the patient is referred from one specialist to another attempting to meet the patient's need by focusing the highly specialized knowledge of different medical practitioners. Lloyd-Jones believed that education could not fully work in this manner, and she saw college student affairs workers as catalysts for bringing about a fuller measure of learning. The dualistic pattern of education has continued into the present. Institutions of higher learning have continued to grow larger and more complex. In the process, campus environments have fractionalized, with many of their units becoming isolated from one another.

One result of this development has been the loss of unified institutional efforts to achieve learning experiences and outcomes for students attending these institutions.

A major change in thinking, however, began as early as the 1960s and marked a shift from emphasis on teaching to emphasis on learning (Straub and Vermilye, 1968). This shift has been a major factor in gradually creating a more favorable climate for student affairs staff and faculty to work together to achieve defined and measurable learning outcomes. Student affairs professionals are presently in a good position to influence learning both in and out of the classroom. To succeed in this role, they will need to develop and apply their skills to the fullest possible degree as learning consultants for college campuses.

The Role of Student Learning Consultants

A basic assumption of this chapter is that learning occurs as a result of a person interacting with an environment (sometimes called a landscape) and receiving feedback about the result of this interaction. As a person is always a part of some landscape and responding to it, there is an ongoing process of reinforcing what has been learned before and achieving new learning mediated primarily by the degree of awareness the person maintains to the available feedback. College students participate in formally organized groups whose mission is to educate, "to provide schooling for," to instruct in specified areas of knowledge that will lead to a certificate of satisfactory completion usually called a degree. Instruction is provided to this end by knowledge specialists called faculty who have themselves been certified in their specialty areas of knowledge with degrees and other criteria of achievement (for example, publications in their knowledge specialty). Skill in teaching, however, is not always required.

The primary premise of this chapter is that college student affairs professionals need to be consultants to the campus community to enhance student learning. A consultant is defined as someone who gives professional advice or services. This requires that to consult a person will have special knowledge in the area in question. Student affairs professionals need to be well versed in knowledge about how students learn and sufficiently skilled in their ability to consult with faculty, students, and other members of the educational community about student learning to facilitate closing the gap between the classroom experience and the out-of-classroom experience. Student affairs staff need to be well grounded in their institution's mission, history, and philosophy. They need to be able to sharpen the focus of this mission and translate its meaning into day-by-day learning opportunities that students can experience all around them. They need to discover and know educational resources that are available for use by faculty and students to enhance progress toward well-defined learning outcomes. These are skills and knowledge recognized as important by the American College Personnel Association (1994) in *The Student Learning Imperative: Implications for Student Affairs*. Even more to the point, perhaps, is the recognition that people are walking social systems who do not experience learning without reflecting on their own behavior and without keeping aware of the degree to which they are responsible for contributing to and reinforcing the consequences of their own behavior (Argyris, 1992).

Consultation for the Whole Campus

To work effectively as learning consultants on the campus, student affairs staff must establish their credibility as people who can help when the need arises. When their skills are requested in the educational community, intervening as team players rather than simply as in-and-out experts will be more often successful. When it can be established that everyone has something to gain in the process, receptivity to working together increases. Student affairs consultants must earn respect for their knowledge of student culture and institutional history. They must be aware of the political forces affecting the campus landscape locally and nationally. Equally important, they must recognize the limits of their own knowledge and expertise and refer to other sources or bring in other individuals with the appropriate knowledge and skills when needed.

Assessment and Research. To succeed as in-house resident consultants on campus, student affairs divisions need to establish, if they do not already have in existence, a major assessment and research arm that will provide up-to-date information about the campus landscape and the changing needs of students. This information can be communicated to the campus community, particularly the faculty, as part of the consulting role of student affairs staff to remove barriers and structural impediments to collaborating to improve effective teaching and learning. Indeed, the continuing development of knowledge about college students, the campus landscape, and how students function on this landscape is the foundation for student affairs professional performance as effective consultants.

Assessment goals that can be transformed into concrete, precise questions are necessary. A method to answer well-defined questions and measures of outcomes can be devised. Such methods will often employ standardized measures that are available with high reliability and validity, such as those provided by the American College Testing Program or the Educational Testing Service. Other sources can be found in the various editions of the *Mental Measurements Yearbook* or reported in the several journals in the field of student affairs and the field of measurement, such as the *Journal of College Student Development* and *Educational and Psychological Measurement*. Tinsley and Ireland (1989) review a number of instruments used for research in the field of college student affairs that may also be valuable for evaluating program outcomes. Posner and Brodsky (1992) present a measure of leadership development, which is a good example of what may be found in the literature to help with consulting in this area.

Ready-made instruments may not always measure the outcomes necessary to answer the specific question posed, however, in which case the student affairs professional will be required to construct new ones. Specialists in the area of measurement may need to be sought for help with this task. In certain cases, qualitative measures can provide the most effective responses (for example, see Lincoln and Guba, 1985; Patton, 1990).

Programs for assessment and measures of outcomes will miss their mark and fail to answer the questions being raised unless they are carefully planned and executed. Time and money can be expended for naught without careful planning. As many representatives of the campus community as possible should be involved in identifying and defining questions to be answered, whereas the execution may be better left to a few individuals well trained in the areas.

Constructing Learning Communities. Particularly in larger institutions, the concept of community may be only an illusion. Various units, both in academic areas and in student affairs, may have become isolated and resistant to collaborative efforts or even obstructive of one another in their competitive efforts.

Information obtained about the particular learning landscape and its inhabitants can be used by student affairs staff to consult with one another and with faculty to forge a common purpose and make the day-by-day activities of the various units reinforce the learning efforts of the entire community. This is a difficult task, particularly in large institutions where the curriculum and faculty have become heavily specialized and fragmented. Many, if not most, students experience only a small segment of the academic community and have little or no sense of the larger institution. Student affairs staff can use their special knowledge and skills to help develop and highlight a variety of natural centers within the educational community where students and faculty can come together for shared purposes to enhance the educational experience and where each person may gain a sense of identity. These centers may be academic departments or entire colleges within universities. They may be activities that have a special significance for a particular campus community or they may be developed within student residence facilities. But they need to be places where students and faculty can achieve their primary educational identity, and they need to be places that can be held responsible for enhancing student learning.

Student Peer Groups. One of the most effective areas to develop and consult with is student groups that work as peer consultants or paraprofessionals. A number of student affairs areas (such as residence halls, career centers, women's centers, learning centers, and counseling centers) use student peer assistants or paraprofessionals. Wellness programs and student health services also use peer groups to assist in their educational work. Although the roles of peer paraprofessionals will vary from campus to campus, the following principles are important on all campus landscapes: establish clear, well-defined roles for peer groups; select participants by carefully constructed criteria; and train participants well for their defined roles (see Ender and Carranza, 1991; Tindall, 1995). Training needs to be planned on a long-term basis

(Mann, 1994). There are legal implications that are important considerations as well. In addition to defined roles, careful selection, and sound training, supervision by appropriate professionals will go a long way in providing a safeguard against litigation. If student peer programs are to be effective, student affairs staff, faculty, and administrators need to be involved with planning, selection, training, and implementation.

Most of the recent research indicates that peer teaching and peer tutorial programs have a positive influence on learning (Pascarella and Terenzini, 1991). Peer advising in orientation programs has been used to foster students' satisfaction with and involvement in the broader academic community (Russel and Skinkle, 1990).

Conflict Resolution. Conflict may occur both in the classroom and outside the classroom. It may result in the need to work with teachers around behavior difficulties and classroom management, or it may result in working directly with difficult students and their needs. Sexual harassment and racial conflicts may be the focus. There is a need to know how to facilitate learning from the conflict that inevitably occurs in every group and community.

Few conflicts are intrinsically and inevitably win-lose situations, however (Deutsch, 1985). There is value in training to help people maintain an awareness of their common needs even as they deal with their opposing interests. It is essential to encourage a cooperative problem-solving orientation, one that focuses on the interests of the different parties and not their positions and uses a communication process that is open, honest, and mutually respectful.

Fogg (1985) described six variable components for categorizing "creative, peaceful approaches" for resolving conflicts that are useful in conceptualizing a strategy: the parties, bases of conflict, location, timing, nature of involvement, and causes. A number of social scientists have supported bringing disputants together in informal small-group workshops under the direction of a third party who is mutually respected (Hare and Naveh, 1985; White, 1986). Knowledge and skill in mediating and adjudicating conflicts with particular attention to their educational outcomes is of great value to student affairs professionals either as they participate directly in resolving a conflict or consult with those who are doing so.

The preferred mode of intervention may vary with the magnitude and intensity of a conflict. The effectiveness of a third party in conflict resolution will vary, of course, depending upon a variety of motivational circumstances. Some conflicts involve a group versus an individual and inevitably raise an issue of the "most good" outcome. The consultant-facilitator who can create and maintain a win-win focus rather than a win-lose focus will more often succeed in resolving conflict. The ultimate goal is to create learning opportunities and outcomes from everyday happenings. As May (1975) so aptly pointed out, "creativity occurs in an act of encounter and is to be understood with this encounter as its center" (p. 87).

Student Activity Transcript and Portfolio. Consultation with students may achieve meaning more easily by using an organizing approach. One consistent and evolving mode with which to work with students is to help them develop an activities transcript or career portfolio. The transcript can be seen as a part of a portfolio. The portfolio has great breadth and potential for illuminating the student's total development. The portfolio is not only a useful tool for students to learn about assessing their personal development through college but is of immense value as they participate in the work world after college. It helps the students to assess their own strengths and weaknesses realistically and to present a balanced picture of themselves to others who are seeking their talents.

Forrest (1990) does an excellent job of describing the use of a portfolio for evaluating general education programs and lists a number of institutions that have experimented with this approach. One of the real strengths of using the portfolio is the tremendous opportunity it provides for collaboration with both students and faculty (Edgerton, Hutchings, and Quinlan, 1991). It is a means of advancing student learning in writing and learning to consult with others as part of the portfolio development process. Decisions that need to be made in this process include defining the nature of the program of learning, deciding what is to be included in the portfolio, building an ongoing and consistent method of developing the portfolio that is time efficient, and establishing ways to help the students get started. Students need help in determining who to collaborate with (and how to use the feedback thus obtained). Student affairs professionals can be advocates for the use of such methods and use their skills and opportunities for consulting with both students and faculty.

Faculty Development and Student Learning

Data gathered in the survey conducted to guide this sourcebook indicate that 63 percent of the student affairs respondents were involved in faculty development programs. This involvement included training academic advisers, coadvising projects with faculty, participating in evaluation of advising programs and improvement of these programs, training and orienting student advisers, assisting with the training of academic tutors, and assisting with the development of mentoring programs and the selection and training of mentors. The survey indicates that many campuses provide opportunities for faculty to consider active learning techniques, teaching and learning environments, collaborative learning approaches, learning skills, learning styles, teaching styles, and Great Teachers seminars, to name some of the most frequently mentioned. It is important for student affairs professionals to be involved in these activities as participants along with faculty. The result can be a greater rapport and increased confidence in developing a working relationship between student affairs consultants and faculty.

The Wakonse Program. The Wakonse Foundation (Johnston, 1994) at the University of Missouri, Columbia, exemplifies this approach. *Wakonse* is a word from the Lakota Indian language meaning to teach, to inspire. The foundation sponsors (among several projects) the Wakonse Conference on College Teaching, which brings together people in a setting designed to display and discuss teaching talents, and to learn about themselves as teachers. In an enjoyable outdoor setting, participants consider teaching in a creative manner. They give and receive feedback from one another as a norm and return to their campuses with the goal of establishing a more supportive climate for those concerned with good teaching. Participants are selected from several institutions by academic deans and department chairs, and they become Wakonse Fellows upon completion of this week-long experience. A Wakonse Fellow is defined as a person committed to inspiring self and others to support, promote, and share the excitement and satisfaction of teaching.

During the past several years, representatives from the division of student affairs at the University of Missouri, Columbia, have been included as participants in the conference with the opportunity to share equally in the excitement of participating and developing their own skills as master teachers. One of the ingredients of the success of this program is the opportunity to begin a process of reconsidering the challenge of teaching outside the institutional structure, where rank and titles have little meaning. Upon their return to campus, participants find that the shared experience provides a bond and connection for continued communication and support in the pursuit of teaching excellence.

The Wakonse Residence. A Wakonse program has recently been initiated to establish a section of the residence halls called the Wakonse Residence designed to stimulate intellectual excitement among undergraduate students that occupy three co-ed floors and are closely monitored by fellows from the Wakonse Teaching Program. Fellows provide special seminars and opportunities for interaction with the students in this area. Students are selected for this living area beginning with an informal written essay on why they are requesting to live in this community and how they may contribute to it. This Wakonse Resident Community is providing students with opportunities for academic and career exploration, and with collaborative research projects with Wakonse Fellows and mentors that may result in academic credit and informal presentations in the living area. The area now includes seminar rooms, study spaces, a computer laboratory, and a career annex for this group. It requires the cooperative efforts of both faculty and student affairs staff working equally to support this community.

Adjustment Behaviors. Faculty may be confronted in the classroom with student behaviors that they feel unprepared to deal with and that go beyond the educative efforts needed to change attitudes and perceptions important to conflict resolution. When this occurs, instructors may not do anything until the conflict gets out of hand and becomes disruptive or even harmful to the individual student and other students involved. Adjustment behaviors may be the result of emotional difficulty or of physical or mental impairment. Emotional and mental problems are among the leading reasons students do not succeed. In the effort to promote student success, emotionally impaired students should be of as much concern as academically impaired students. Faculty very often do not know who to talk to or where to look for help with this problem.

The first challenge confronting an instructor is identifying the problem. The nature of the problem will determine the response required from the institution. Faculty can be helped to recognize signs of potential problems such as poor listening or discussion skills. Other signs of potential problems are social incompetence, interpersonal insensitivity, and boundary violations. Knowing when and how to refer students for help may save their academic careers, but faculty seldom have knowledge or training in this area.

Learning Disabilities. Another problem population that is growing in importance consists of students with learning disabilities. Faculty will need help to determine the type and degree of accommodation each student with a learning disability will require to perform successfully in a course. In responding to impaired students, faculty must work under the dictates of the 1990 Americans with Disabilities Act, which requires public institutions to provide "reasonable accommodation" for students with disabilities.

Each institution needs to establish clear policy on how it responds to both physically and learning-impaired students. It must designate the person or persons responsible for interpreting and administering its policy. Student affairs divisions should have staff who are capable of training faculty, consulting with faculty, and administering programs in this area if need be.

Working with Faculty

Faculty are not the enemy. They are not necessarily on the other side of a competitive contest. Although they usually prize their autonomy and independence, they are heavily influenced by the reward system in academia and the goals of succeeding as a part of an academic discipline. What is known from research and experience about changing the way people perform their roles indicates that it may be best to allow faculty what they need in accordance with how they define themselves, which is usually strongly influenced by their academic discipline. Faculty need to be allowed to seek assistance within the framework of their own definition. The knowledge and expertise that student affairs professionals have about students and the campus environment can work well within this framework to achieve desirable learning outcomes for students. It will not succeed, however, if faculty and student affairs professionals perform their roles as if they exist on two separate landscapes or as if they are competing for dominance on a single landscape. Providing leadership to bring about meetings with faculty to discuss learning issues, to share data that can affect practice both in and out of the classroom, and to create workshops and special demonstrations to consider teaching skills and learning outcomes and the use of new technology in the classroom are but a few of the ways to strengthen a collaborative role and to share the effort to improve opportunities for student learning.

A first step may be to encourage classroom instructors to experiment with new approaches to teaching in the classroom. Most individuals are more willing to experiment with new approaches and change their methods within a framework in which they feel secure. After experiencing success in a comfortable setting, they will be more willing to venture further afield. A second step may be to encourage faculty who have been successful working with students in their own disciplines to attempt cross-disciplinary projects. Typically, faculty are housed in disciplinary groupings located in separate buildings in separate areas of the campus. Schedules may not facilitate much interaction between faculty members and when interaction does occur it may not focus on teaching and student learning. Student affairs professionals can position themselves to stimulate faculty cross-disciplinary interaction and discussion that will lead to new learning opportunities for students. Cross-disciplinary learning can be particularly beneficial in the first two years of college. The experience of seeing faculty from different academic disciplines interact can be an exciting and productive experience for students and may even be cost-effective.

Preparation for the Consulting Role

How does a person prepare to fulfill the role discussed in this chapter? There are no graduate programs that achieve this goal nor should they be expected to do so any more than they can be expected to deliver a new graduate competent to immediately occupy the role of a chief student affairs officer. But they can and in some instances do lay the foundation. More needs to be done to build expectations for developing the knowledge and skills important to fulfilling this role on campus, however. More needs to be done in preparation programs to prepare student affairs professionals to understand and work effectively with the unique landscapes that each institution presents. More needs to be done to teach about how students of all ages learn at both a cognitive and affective level. In the final analysis, however, it will depend upon each student affairs professional to continuously prepare for and practice the science and art of fulfilling the role along with the other tasks of their specific assignment.

Summary

Colleges and universities have always focused on student learning. The never-ceasing debate is about the nature of learning; what should be learned and how should it be achieved. Whether it is a parent instructing a child or a professor working with college students, the nature of learning, its content, and its purpose are always relative to its context. Arguments are developed to justify actions. These arguments always reflect norms and values that reflect their social and cultural grounding. Dewey (1916) declared, "It is the very nature of life to strive to continue in being," adding that "life is a self-renewing process" and that of necessity "every social arrangement is educative in effect" (p. 9).

The Student Learning Imperative: Implications for Student Affairs (American College Personnel Association, 1994) is a clear call for rededication to the mission and values of college student affairs. The statement is particularly important for the way it reflects the present social and economic context of the landscape on which higher education is striving for life. The need for faculty, students, student affairs staff, and other administrators to collaborate to achieve a more relevant and higher-quality education has never been greater. Student affairs professionals have the expertise to provide needed leadership in this process. The role of consultant needs to be a highly developed part of this expertise. The values that underlie the profession and its practice must be continually evaluated to maintain its self-renewing abilities. Consulting can be a valuable service to others in the campus community and valuable to the profession's own self-renewing process.

References

American College Personnel Association. *The Student Learning Imperative: Implications for Student Affairs.* Washington, D.C.: American College Personnel Association, 1994.

Argyris, C. *On Organizational Learning.* Cambridge, Mass.: Blackwell, 1992.

Deutsch, M. *Distributive Justice: A Social-Psychological Perspective.* New Haven, Conn.: Yale University Press, 1985.

Dewey, J. *Democracy and Education: An Introduction to the Philosophy of Education.* New York: Macmillan, 1916.

Edgerton, R., Hutchings, P., and Quinlan, K. *The Teaching Portfolio.* Washington, D.C.: American Association of Higher Education, 1991.

Ender, S. C., and Carranza, C. "Students as Paraprofessionals." In T. K. Miller, R. B. Winston, Jr., and Associates, *Administration and Leadership in Student Affairs.* (2nd ed.) Muncie, Ind.: Accelerated Development, 1991.

Fogg, R. W. "Dealing with Conflict: A Repertoire of Creative, Peaceful Approaches." *Journal of Conflict Resolution,* 1985, *29,* 330–358.

Forrest, A. *Time Will Tell: Portfolio-Assisted Assessment of General Education.* Washington, D.C.: American Association of Higher Education, 1990.

Hare, A. P., and Naveh, D. "Creative Problem Solving: Camp David Summit, 1978." *Small Group Behavior,* 1985, *16,* 123–138.

Johnston, J. "Wakonse Program." Program brochure. Columbia: University of Missouri, 1994.

Lincoln, V. S., and Guba, E. G. *Naturalistic Inquiry.* Thousand Oaks, Calif.: Sage, 1985.

Lloyd-Jones, E., and Smith, M. R. (eds.). *Student Personnel Work as Deeper Teaching.* New York: HarperCollins, 1954.

Mann, A. F. "College Peer Tutoring Journals: Maps of Development." *Journal of College Student Development,* 1994, *35,* 164–169.

May, R. *The Courage to Create.* New York: Bantam, 1975.

Pascarella, E. T., and Terenzini, P. T. *How College Affects Students: Findings and Insights from Twenty Years of Research.* San Francisco: Jossey-Bass, 1991.

Patton, M. Q. *Qualitative Evaluation and Research Methods.* (2nd ed.) Thousand Oaks, Calif.: Sage, 1990.

Posner, B. Z., and Brodsky, B. "A Leadership Development Instrument for College Students." *Journal of College Student Development,* 1992, *33,* 231–237.

Russel, J. H., and Skinkle, K. R. "Evaluation of Peer-Advisor Effectiveness." *Journal of College Student Development,* 1990, *31,* 388–394.

Straub, J. S., and Vermilye, D. W. "Current and Developing Issues in Student Life." *Journal of College Student Personnel*, 1968, *9*, 363–370.

Tindall, J. A. *Peer Programs: An In-Depth Look at Peer-Helping*. Bristol, Pa.: Accelerated Development, 1995.

Tinsley, D. J., and Ireland, T. M. "Instruments Used in College and Student Affairs Research: An Analysis of the Measurement Base of a Young Profession." *Journal of College Student Development*, 1989, *30*, 440–447.

White, R. K. (ed.). *Psychology and the Prevention of Nuclear War*. New York: New York University Press, 1986.

RICHARD B. CAPLE is director of the Counseling Center and professor of education at the University of Missouri–Columbia.

Within the context of the community college, student affairs programs designed to support student success and learning are explored. Ten expectations for a comprehensive, learning-oriented student affairs program are suggested.

Student Affairs in the Community College: Promoting Student Success and Learning

Kenneth L. Ender, Sunil Chand, Jerry Sue Thornton

As described in Chapter One, significant changes are occurring in higher education across the country. The focus is shifting from developing environments that support teaching to ones that support learning. In these emerging environments the message is clear: students *matter* (Schlossberg, Lynch, and Chickering, 1989) and student success is the institution's top priority.

In the community college context, Astin's characterization of success as students persisting to goal completion is most appropriate (1982). Success involves something different for each community college student. For some it means transferring to another institution, for others attaining an associate degree, certificate, or additional training; and yet for others it may simply mean gaining confidence in the postsecondary setting or pursuing an interest related to a personal development agenda.

Given these multiple student agendas, the community college must develop and maintain an ongoing relationship with its students so that their goals are known, encouraged, and monitored. In most cases, the community college will be unable to gauge the success of its students simply by looking at the traditional measure of graduation rates. For most, this would give a highly distorted and unrealistic appraisal. Student goal attainment and the learning necessary to meet these goals must be continually measured and monitored for the college to have a clear picture of its impact on the student body and the community in which it resides. This demands that all personnel and resources of the institution work together to monitor and assure student success.

Traditionally, student services have functioned separately from academic services and the teaching faculty. However, in the community college setting this is no longer a viable model. If student success is to be understood and achieved, it is essential that student and academic services work as a team fostering a holistic and comprehensive educational environment in which students can excel.

The Community College Setting

In 1995, there were 1,112 public and private community colleges in the United States, enrolling over 5.5 million students (American Association of Community Colleges, 1995). Community colleges are primarily open-access institutions enrolling all that desire a higher education and hold the high school degree or equivalent.

Community college students, the new majority, if you will, are older, typically attend part time, and present needs, expectations, and lifestyles vastly different from those of traditional undergraduates at the four-year residential institution (Gilley and Hawkes, 1989). This new majority of students have changed "forever the profile of higher education in America. Today, only 42 percent of America's higher education students are considered traditional—that is, students under twenty-five who attend a four-year institution full-time" (Martens, Lara, Cordova, and Harris, 1995, p. 5). In this new majority one finds underprepared students, reentry women, midlife career changers, students of color, physically challenged students, and nonnative English speakers.

In most four-year residential colleges, many students enrolled at the community college would be labeled at risk. However, *at risk* in the community college has taken on a new meaning. Roueche and Roueche (1993) have extended the label to students who are not only academically underprepared, but also work thirty or more hours a week, have little support from family members, are first generation to attend college, and have developed expectations of failure. As these risk factors are considered, coupled with the diversity of students and their widely differentiated goals, the community college setting becomes both complex and challenging for the student affairs community, whose goal is to promote student learning and success. A creative and multidimensional programming response is mandated in this complex learning environment.

Issues Affecting Student Learning

As students enter, proceed through, and move away from the institution, they present the college with particular personal and individual issues that influence the organization of resources. Some of these issues demand a highly personalized response; others can be met through technology. There are at least five major issues that require a planned response from the community college.

Many of these institutional interventions will require leadership from student affairs professionals.

Joining the institution. Being quite different from the traditional college student, the new student at the community college brings a number of learning needs upon first joining. These needs have little to do with the curriculum, and are instead germane to individual concerns in the context of the nature and scope of the institution. The institution will therefore want to help students find out about the institution of higher education, the resources available at a particular institution, and whether or not there is a fit between the student's interests and the resources and culture of the particular institution the student is attending.

Achieving academic success. Students will need assistance, support, and validation (Ratcliff and Assoc., 1995) that higher education is the right choice and that there is a high probability of success. Issues of appropriate placement in courses, where to find learning resources and support, and documenting progress will all be important to assuring the success of the student.

Becoming affiliated and involved. The correlation between student affiliation and involvement in learning and subsequent persistence to goal attainment is well documented (Tinto and Kadel, 1994). Students will seek reference and identity groups in which to become affiliated. Becoming acquainted with faculty members will be an important yet, for some, difficult objective.

Maximizing personal potential. Adult development issues will face all students. For some this will be an important time in life to seek answers to identity questions developing personal congruence between life goals and a current career or degree objective. Others will discover or perhaps rediscover their interest in leadership or sponsorship of ideas and causes. For all students, the college experience provides the opportunity to set a goal and meet it.

Completing educational objectives. Tracking progress and performance is an important objective for the student. Progress reports and documentation of accomplishments is essential. Being assured that course work taken at the college is transferable to baccalaureate degree programs is critical. Moving along the academic career ladder from noncredit to credit-bearing courses is vitally important for some. Receiving a credential, which signals to others that success has been attained, is critical to the support of community college students.

Organizing Resources

Student affairs programs must organize their resources to respond to these student issues so that the probability of student success and learning is maximized. Organization of resources can be arranged by a consideration of the seven key functions that the League of Innovation in the Community College (O'Banion, 1987) has postulated as necessary for assuring student success. Each is listed in this section, with suggestions about what student affairs programs must do to provide the function described.

Define processes for student intake, monitor progress, and document student outcomes. Student affairs programs must develop appropriate institutional policies, programs, and procedures that require orientation, assessment, course placement, and educational planning. Processes must be in place to provide effective and efficient registration and enrollment processes that are convenient for students and use appropriate technology. The student affairs program must assist in implementing processes that monitor student progress, measure student outcomes, and evaluate the effectiveness of programs and services for students.

Develop processes that encourage student association and involvement with the college. Programs must be in place to encourage and assist in creating opportunities for student, faculty, and other staff interaction both in and outside the classroom. Student affairs programs must promote student interaction and involvement with all aspects of student life and the campus activities program.

Provide a full range and schedule of services to permit students to benefit from college programs. Student support services—such as orientation, counseling, assessment, educational planning, financial aid, and the like must be scheduled to serve all students, whether they attend by day or in the evening, full or part time, for credit or not, and weekdays or weekends.

Prescribe and provide programs that assure student competence in specified academic and skill areas. Student affairs staff must recommend and participate in the development of programs that assure student competence in general skills, general education, and preparation for further education. Programs must be developed and enforced that assure student success, including policies on class attendance, grading, course loads, and minimum academic progress.

Coordinate programs with secondary schools, other colleges, universities, and business and industry. Student affairs programs must assist in developing and maintaining program articulation agreements with both secondary schools and four-year colleges and universities. Programs must be in place to assist transfer students. A comprehensive program of career planning and placement must be in place.

Use state-of-the-art technology to increase the efficiency and effectiveness of services provided to students to prepare them for productive lives in an increasingly technological society. A program of student information that provides educational planning, progress monitoring, prescription of intervention strategies (degree audits, early warning systems, minimum academic progress checks, and so on) must be developed with participation from student affairs.

Develop and implement long-range hiring plans and comprehensive staff development programs to assure that all college staff possess the competence required to help students succeed in their educational pursuits. Student affairs programs must constantly identify the skills, competencies, characteristics, and attitudes required of successful student affairs practitioners. Staff development programs must be aimed at assuring that student affairs staff possess skills consistent with facilitating student success.

Developing a Comprehensive Student Affairs Program

As illustrated, many student affairs programs are promoting student learning and success through a variety of interventions. However, for the most part these activities are not associated with classroom learning and are occurring separately from those learning activities moderated by the faculty. In fact, it is not uncommon to find these student affairs–sponsored services and activities being provided in traditional ways as modeled by residential universities. As student success and learning is embraced as the essential organizational model, student affairs must consider innovative strategies for organizing and working with the faculty to assure student success. An organizational model and service delivery system must be developed with that end in mind.

Such a comprehensive student affairs program mandates the delivery of a strongly integrated and dynamic array of services that are aligned with the academic administrative areas and the faculty. A program of this nature is intended to develop institutional and personal behaviors, a culture if you will, that is student centered and committed to the success of each student. Programs with these characteristics integrate the talents, resources, and energies of the academic and student affairs communities to provide a relevant and holistic college experience for students.

From Theory to Practice

Cuyahoga Community College is developing a student-centered culture by promulgating a set of expectations for its student affairs program that is comprehensive and designed to support student success and learning (Ender and others, 1995). The origins of these expectations are clearly supported in the professional literature describing student affairs and its relationship to student learning (American College Personnel Association, 1994; American Council on Education, 1937; Helfgot and Culp, 1995; Culp, 1995a, 1995b; Kuh, Lyons, Miller, and Trow, 1994; O'Banion, 1987; Astin and others, 1984; Ratcliff and Assoc., 1995; and Wingspread Group on Higher Education, 1993). Many of the exemplary programs and best practices found within community colleges across the country (Becherer and Becherer, 1995) characterize these expectations.

Student affairs staff provide leadership for the development of a student-centered environment throughout the college. Student-centered environments are characterized by persons demonstrating a sense of civility and respect for others. The environment is educationally stimulating. Planners of college processes intentionally include students in their work and strive to increase contact among students, faculty, and administrators. The services of the college are aligned with student availability, and students are viewed and interacted with holistically, not just intellectually. Mass customization techniques in the delivery of student services are in place so that each student receives personalized service.

Student affairs staff advocate for the success of all students. This advocacy assures that student opinions and needs are solicited and expressed in the development of college policies and practices. A full range of services are provided to support student success. Students attending the college know that they matter. Each student has an advocate for his or her success and the student affairs staff aggressively advocate for the elimination of barriers that may limit student success.

Student affairs staff collaborate with instructional faculty to ensure student success. Collaboration with faculty provides information to them about students, the institution, its resources, and teaching and learning. Student affairs staff engage the faculty as a participant group of the student affairs program and assist the faculty in their roles as mentors and advocates for student success. With the faculty, the student affairs program develops academic cocurricular activities that promote social as well as intellectual involvement for students, accentuating greater levels of interaction between faculty and students. Programs, systems, and services are in place to assist the faculty with rigorously assessing what their students know and are able to do, so as to improve both student and institutional performance.

Student affairs staff manage an array of enrollment services that ensure student access and smooth transition through the college's enrollment and matriculation processes. The enrollment services program uses applicable technology and encourages appropriate human contact for course selection and educational planning. Student information systems are in place, including automated student records, centralized advisement information, programs of study, and degree audits. The staff facilitate appropriate involvement and cooperation of the student's family in the college transition process. A financial aid program will be in place to appropriately assure access while maximizing available resources for those most able to benefit. Potential students are provided with consumer-oriented information related to costs early in the decision-making process. In addition, student affairs staff study enrollment patterns in relation to area demographics and contribute this information to marketing plans.

Student affairs staff direct and manage a student advising and counseling program that appropriately challenges students to succeed. The advising and counseling program places students into appropriate sequences of courses that suit their current skills and educational objectives. It develops a comprehensive program of personalized support for students. The program integrates career counseling, educational services, and information resources, assisting each student in defining realistic educational and career objectives. Systems are in place to monitor students' progress toward their stated goals, and these systems include regular instructional faculty and staff contact with students to provide intervention and assistance. Students receive ongoing and timely feedback regarding their progress. Counselors assist students with addressing personal issues that may impede their ability to succeed and coordinate services with outside community agencies, including economic, medical, rehabilitation, and other social services.

Student affairs staff ensure that first-time students in higher education receive special attention and support. Programs for first-time students are front-loaded and integrate the services of admissions, orientation, assessment and course placement, academic and career counseling and advising, early-warning academic alert systems, and mentor programs. Information systems are in place to identify who is recruited and admitted and determine whether there is a fit between student needs and available support systems. A strong retention program is in place. Ongoing research identifies those who persist, drop out, or fail and strive to identify successful intervention practices.

Student affairs staff ensure appropriate educational interventions for students who are not likely to meet their educational objectives. Students who typically do not meet their educational objectives are defined and known by a set of identifying characteristics. Appropriate programs of support are assured through accurate assessment, mandatory course placement, and referral to tutorial, financial, and other aid offices. Tracking systems are in place to provide intrusive early interventions in collaboration with instructional faculty for students not meeting their objectives.

Student affairs staff facilitate a program of student involvement that encourages institutional community building through student and faculty interaction. A program of campus community building is nurtured and developed by collaboration with the instructional faculty to create cocurricular activities, programs, and organizations to increase the students' affiliation with the college and bring added relevance to each student's program of study. Opportunities are created for interaction among students, faculty, and staff inside and outside the classroom. Student involvement is facilitated through programs and activities designed to develop strong student reference groups and identity with the college.

Student affairs staff develop and disseminate information about students to faculty, policymakers, and other college service agencies that assist with developing programs, policies, and practices assuring student success. A student information system is maintained that informs the faculty and staff about the institution's students in the aggregate, by cohort and reference groups, and by each individual student. This information may include social-demographic data, profiles of those who succeed and those who do not, and information about each student's goals, learning styles, learning impediments, interests, family background, previous educational experiences, strengths, and responsibilities external to the college. Student affairs staff monitor changing student needs, as documented locally, regionally, and nationally, for use in program planning and support service development. It is the staff's responsibility to also provide ongoing information regarding student success after exit, in four-year programs, jobs, career tracks, and community involvement.

Student affairs staff provide information regarding the ongoing assessment of their staff, programs, practices, and policies and document how they contribute to student success. Assessment processes are implemented and maintained to evaluate the effectiveness of student affairs programs and services and demonstrate how they improve as a result of evaluation. Staff document that student affairs programs are constantly tested, and continue to demonstrate, through data, how student affairs work adds value to student learning and student success. A current inventory of the skills and knowledge base available within the student affairs staff is maintained, demonstrating the organization's capacity to facilitate student affairs outcomes. A professional development program is in place that documents how staff competencies are consistent with changing student and institutional needs.

Students Define Success

Students meeting their own goals define success in the community college setting. For community colleges to know if they are successful, a keen understanding of their students' intentions is critical. This chapter has developed the rationale for a much closer connection between student affairs professionals and those in academic services, particularly the teaching faculty. This partnership is essential if student learning is to be enhanced and student success assured. The expectations of the Cuyahoga program provide a clear set of evaluative criteria for those student affairs programs attempting to respond to the call to enhance student success and learning and improve learning conditions in the postsecondary setting. It is a set of expectations that has been driven by the goal of developing a comprehensive student affairs program intentionally supporting student learning. Programs reflecting these expectations view both students and faculty as the primary client base and work aggressively to link with these constituencies in educationally meaningful ways. In programs driven by these expectations, the student affairs staff are involved in a dynamic partnership with all those involved in teaching and learning.

References

American Association of Community Colleges. *Pocket Profile of Community Colleges: Trends and Statistics, 1995–96.* Washington, D.C.: American Association of Community Colleges, 1995.

American College Personnel Association. *The Student Learning Imperative: Implications for Student Affairs.* Washington, D.C.: American College Personnel Association, 1994.

American Council on Education. *The Student Personnel Point of View.* Washington, D.C.: American Council on Education, 1937.

Astin, A. W. *Minorities in American Higher Education: Recent Trends, Current Prospects, and Recommendations.* San Francisco: Jossey-Bass, 1982.

Astin, A. W., and others. *Involvement in Learning: Realizing the Potential of American Higher Education.* Washington, D.C.: National Institute of Education, Department of Education, 1984.

Becherer, J. J., and Becherer, J. "Programs, Services, and Activities: A Survey of the Community College Landscape." In S. R. Helfgot and M. Culp (eds.), *Promoting Student Success in the Community College.* New Directions for Student Services, no. 69. San Francisco: Jossey-Bass, 1995.

Culp, M. "Building Bridges: A Team Approach to Transforming Student Services in the Community College." In G. A. Baker (ed.), *Team Building for Quality: Transitions in the*

American Community College. Washington, D.C.: American Association of Community Colleges, 1995a.

Culp, M. "Organizing for Student Success." In S. R. Helfgot and M. Culp (eds.), *Promoting Student Success in the Community College.* New Directions for Student Services, no. 69. San Francisco: Jossey-Bass, 1995b.

Ender, K. L., Bishop, I., Brisker, L., Hripko-Jacob, K., Jones, E., Key, R., McNulty, J., Moss, R., Ross, P., and Schick, T. *Student Affairs: A Comprehensive Program, the Mission and Outcomes.* Cleveland: Cuyahoga Community College, 1995.

Gilley, J. W., and Hawkes, R. T. "Nontraditional Students: A Changing Student Body Redefines Community." *Educational Record,* Summer/Fall 1989, pp. 33–35.

Helfgot, S. R., and Culp, M. *Promoting Student Success in the Community College.* New Directions for Student Services, no. 69. San Francisco: Jossey-Bass, 1995.

Kuh, G. D., Lyons, J., Miller, T., and Trow, J. *Reasonable Expectations: Renewing the Educational Compact Between Institutions and Students.* Washington, D.C.: National Association of Student Personnel Administrators, 1994.

Martens, K., Lara, E., Cordova, J., and Harris, H. "Community College Students: Ever Changing, Ever New." In S. R. Helfgot and M. Culp (eds.), *Promoting Student Success in the Community College.* New Directions for Student Services, no. 69. San Francisco: Jossey-Bass, 1995.

O'Banion, T. *Assuring Student Success in the Community College.* Johnson County, Kans.: League of Innovation in the Community College, 1987.

Ratcliff, J. L., and Associates. *Realizing the Potential: Improving Postsecondary Teaching, Learning, and Assessment.* University Park: National Center on Postsecondary Teaching, Learning, and Assessment, University of Pennsylvania, 1995.

Roueche, J. E., and Roueche, S. D. *Between a Rock and a Hard Place.* Washington, D.C.: American Association of Community Colleges, 1993.

Schlossberg, N. K., Lynch, A. Q., and Chickering, A. W. *Improving Higher Education Environments for Adults: Responsive Programs and Services from Entry to Departure.* San Francisco: Jossey-Bass, 1989.

Tinto, V. R., and Kadel, S. "Constructing Educational Communities: Increasing Retention in Challenging Circumstances." *Community College Journal,* 1994, 64 (4), 26–30.

Wingspread Group on Higher Education. *An American Imperative: Higher Expectations for Higher Education.* Racine, Wis.: Wingspread Group on Higher Education, Johnson Foundation, 1993.

KENNETH L. ENDER *is vice president for academic affairs at Richland Community College, Decatur, Illinois.*

SUNIL CHAND *is executive vice president for academic and student affairs at Cuyahoga Community College, Cleveland, Ohio.*

JERRY SUE THORNTON *is president of Cuyahoga Community College, Cleveland, Ohio.*

Orientation programs facilitate the transition and integration of students into the college learning environment. Examples are given to demonstrate the varied aspects of high-quality orientation programs.

Orientation Programs: A Foundation for Student Learning and Success

Debra A. G. Robinson, Carl F. Burns, Kevin F. Gaw

Orientation programs are designed to help students make a successful transition to the college environment and to initiate the process of higher learning. These programs set the tone for student expectations and begin the process of integrating students into the campus culture. Successful orientation programming promotes confidence among matriculating students and their families—confidence that they have selected an appropriate institution that may lead to a successful college experience. This chapter examines the role of orientation programs from a student learning perspective, reviews current orientation programming practices, and describes some exemplary orientation activities in the United States. The review of current practices is based on a program survey recently completed by 273 colleges across the country.

Orientation Program Contributions to Student Learning

Integrating students into the social and academic fabric of the institution is key to their retention and success (Tinto, 1987). Orientation programs facilitate student learning in three general dimensions: transition processes, academic integration, and personal and social integration. Adequate information about the new environment is essential to beginning the transition process. In addition, orientation provides new students the opportunity to meet people in the campus community, to begin planning their professional development, and to establish realistic expectations congruent with those of the institution. Providing opportunities to learn and grow in academic and personal and social dimensions is essential for student adaptation and success. The Council for the Advancement of Standards (1986) highlighted the importance of addressing academic and student life aspects of the institution as foundations for orientation program content.

Transition Processes. Transition to a new environment can produce significant stress. The stress of college adjustment is evident in patterns of college persistence. Almost half of student attrition takes place during the first year (Porter, 1990). Students may drop out of college without giving themselves an adequate chance to adjust. If students do not have a commitment to college, the transitional stress may discourage them from sticking it out (Tinto, 1987). Students need adequate information to begin the transition process and provide a foundation for college learning.

Information helps to reduce stress due to uncertainty and fosters an active problem-solving style, an important life skill. Successful orientation programs provide learning experiences that help students understand and make adaptations to change. College entry is the beginning of a series of life changes, and the better we educate our students to successfully navigate change, the more they learn and grow personally and professionally.

Most orientation programs provide opportunities for new students to become familiar with the campus and learn about campus support services. Students need to know their way around campus to feel comfortable with their new environment. Financial concerns and education costs are also usually dealt with during orientation. Students and their families need to know about education costs and financial aid availability to make good consumer decisions.

Orientation provides an opportunity for incoming students to learn about campus living options. Some programs include an overnight stay in a residence hall. Examining residence hall and Greek life options is an early learning experience for college students, as they can make an informed decision about where to live during their first year of college. Early exposure helps new students conceptualize potential new living environments and helps them learn to make important decisions that will directly affect their lives. Knowledge about living opportunities and active involvement in the decision-making process can reduce anxiety about the unknowns of a new living environment.

A critical part of the educational experience for many students is the involvement of their families in the introduction to college (White, Goetz, Hunter, and Barefoot, 1995). Family members often have many questions and concerns about the college environment. Orientation programs can help parents understand student intellectual and social development, expectations of the campus community, and campus support services. Providing information to significant others can facilitate the transition process for students and parents and ultimately enhance student success in college. Orientation programming can be seen as an invitation to parents to begin their own developmental step of letting go of their children as students and allowing the campus to enter the parenting-mentoring process as a team member.

Integration with the Academic Community. Assisting students with their adjustment to the academic environment is often a primary emphasis of orientation programming. Because of the link to student retention, there has been a trend during the last ten years toward formalizing and marketing orientation programs with a more serious academic tone (Noel, Levitz, Saluri, and Assoc., 1985) and focusing on introducing students to the academic community (Upcraft and Gardner, 1989). According to data from the annual Cooperative Institutional Research Program (CIRP) survey, students often choose institutions based on academic majors offered and academic reputation (Sax, Astin, Korn, and Mahoney, 1995). Hence, it makes sense that students would have a strong desire to obtain information about academic programs and activities to enhance academic success. In spite of these factors, most incoming first-year students are not well prepared to deal with the increased academic expectations they are about to experience.

Activities to facilitate academic adjustment and success typically include both placement and informational components. Academic advising, placement testing, and registration for fall courses are included in most orientation programs. The informational components often comprise information on academic programs, grading policies, graduation requirements, expectations regarding academic conduct, and time and study commitments necessary for academic success.

Academic Information. Academic information is usually disseminated by faculty and academic administrators, providing incoming students and their families an opportunity to meet and interact with faculty and campus administrators. Incoming students need to understand curriculum structure, graduation requirements, grading policies, and general university policies and procedures. Awareness of these rules and procedures is important for learning and academic success.

Students also need to develop realistic expectations of the amount of work required to be academically successful. Each campus is unique in its practices and expectations of students and should make every effort to provide this important information to students prior to actual course enrollment. Academic information needs to be provided in a way that students can comprehend and find meaningful.

The University of Evansville in Evansville, Indiana, addresses academic expectations through their Academic Reality Therapy Program. The presentation, conducted by a panel of faculty and students, includes personal and anecdotal information about academic life. It is followed by departmental meetings with faculty and small-group meetings with student orientation leaders. Parents also meet with a panel of parents of current students.

Illinois State University in Normal, Illinois, offers Classroom 101, a simulated large lecture classroom experience that helps students learn about the expectations of being a college student. Academic honesty, classroom preparation, interaction with faculty, and classroom assistance are discussed. The Classroom 101 experience is coordinated and taught by distinguished university professors. These classroom simulations and group discussions are effective means of helping incoming students appreciate the differential effort necessary for college course work as compared to high school classes. Meeting with experienced students in their intended majors helps new students learn about other student experiences and expectations. Many campuses also address academic survival skills during orientation.

Placement Testing. Academic integration requires placement in the appropriate beginning courses. College campuses use national tests, ACT and SAT scores, and high school grade and rank information for admission purposes. This information can also be used in combination with specialized placement tests, such as the Missouri Mathematics Placement Test, to make course placement decisions for each student. Effective learning and academic success depend upon proper placement. A student mistakenly accelerated in an area of actual deficiency will encounter more difficulties (social *and* academic) and have reduced chances for success compared to an appropriately placed student of the same abilities (White, Goetz, Hunter, and Barefoot, 1995).

Academic Advising. Gardner and Hansen (1993) point out that effective orientation allows new students to begin to develop the all-important relationship with their academic advisers. Faculty can help students understand academic responsibilities and expectations in the classroom and within the academic community. Getting to know faculty and their interpretations of campus expectations can help students develop relationships with faculty and enhance learning and attachment to the campus community. Probably the most important role for faculty in the orientation process is to serve as academic advisers for the incoming students (Frost, 1991; Kramer and Spencer, 1989). An effective academic adviser is knowledgeable about his or her discipline area and campus policies and procedures, and is able to listen to, affirm, and guide students through the educational process. The quality of academic advising is a primary retention factor (Thomas, 1990); however, its importance is often not appreciated in reward systems.

Course Registration. Selecting and registering for fall courses is usually involved in orientation programs at some point. This activity is often the culmination of a prematriculation or early registration program. This is an area of primary interest and concern for incoming freshmen. Students often choose the earliest possible orientation session to relieve their concerns about getting fall classes. Completion of course registration also alleviates some anxiety among new students, freeing them to focus energy on their personal and social integration on campus.

Part of the learning process is understanding the university system for course registration. Campus systems vary, and orientation is the prime opportunity to teach students how to effectively complete registration procedures. This process is something they will continue to execute many times during their undergraduate years; early mastery will heighten their campus experience.

Personal-Social Integration. Orientation must also address student adjustment to the social environment. Students need information about the institution's values, behavioral norms, expectations of community members, and support services, and an appreciation of normal student development issues. This is also a time to raise issues of diversity, alcohol use, acquaintance rape, personal safety, and other student concerns. Information on campus housing alternatives, opportunities for professional development, involvement in student organizations, and service learning can facilitate student transition and connection to the campus.

Orientation programs provide an opportunity for incoming students to become better acquainted with other new students, current students, faculty, and staff. Institutional expectations and student perceptions and expectations can be shared and discussed. Orientation is a community-building experience for the campus; new students should feel a sense of connection and commitment to the campus after participating in an orientation program. Introducing students to professional and peer mentors during orientation can be a particularly effective way to enhance students' academic adjustment, facilitate student learning, and provide an important support system. Astin (1993) observed that two critical factors affecting student retention are the extent to which the student interacts with student peers and with faculty.

Community Building. Community building is an important aspect of many orientation programs. It has been shown that students who feel connected to other students and the campus community are more likely to persist to graduation (Astin, 1993). Orientation is the ideal time to start building these relationships and commitments, and effective programs incorporate active efforts to do so. Most of the orientation programs surveyed incorporate social networking and community-building activities.

Orientation programs offer an opportunity to meet current students and other incoming students. Learning to meet new people and communicate effectively are important personal and professional learning experiences. Interactions with members of the campus community are critical at an early point in a student's college career (Tinto, 1993). Sheets and Zakely (1995) assert that student success is related to the degree to which students feel that they matter, that they belong to the community, and that they are appreciated for who they are and want to become.

Participation in out-of-classroom experiences is important for student learning and development of the whole person. Orientation is a time to showcase the clubs and organizations available to students on campus. Early contact with members of student organizations can be very important for new students trying to decide among the available options. For some students, feeling wanted and a perceived fit may help them decide which organizations they join. Further, merely experiencing club and organization activity, even on an informational basis, helps to develop a sense of community.

Orientation staff members must communicate the importance of cocurricular involvement for professional development. Some new students may be so focused on grades that they are reluctant to join student organizations; they only want to spend time studying. They need to understand that personal and social skills are sought by employers and that simply completing a college degree is no longer sufficient to be marketable in the professional world. It has been well documented that involvement is critical for student persistence and success (Astin, 1993; Pace, 1994). Student involvement in the university community leads to commitment to the university community (Schroeder, Mable, and Assoc., 1994). As individuals become involved, invested, and influential, they begin to identify with and develop their status as members of the community. This process lays the foundation for a learning community and promotes development necessary to a student's professional and personal identity. (Other students, of course, may experience the opposite problem, and want to spend all their time in cocurricular activities. They too need encouragement and assistance in finding a balance.)

To help students become involved in and attached to the campus community, some campuses use team-building retreats or leadership development courses. These programs may include off-campus outdoor functions, activities to increase self-awareness and appreciation of others, and programs to increase interpersonal and leadership skills. Our survey indicates that leadership development programs are frequently included in orientation programs. For example, Bethel College in McKenzie, Tennessee, offers an Outward Bound experience to Natchez Trace State Park and a Leadership Development Course for incoming freshmen immediately before beginning the fall semester.

Campus Expectations. Orientation programs need to provide new students with information about behavioral expectations. This information is one basis for social learning and development of college students. Knowing behavioral norms and limits can resolve areas of uncertainty, freeing students to grow and learn and sparing them the need to expend energy on trying to figure out the rules. Students also need to understand why rules and expectations exist and the consequences for violating limits.

Many campuses are including discussions and activities to address diversity issues. Developing tolerance and appreciation of differences can be a major learning experience during the college years. Students come from myriad social, cultural, geographic, and ethnic backgrounds. Part of their education and professional development is learning to accept and work effectively with people from a wide range of backgrounds. Students need to develop global perspectives to be effective professionals in the twenty-first century.

Student Development Issues. Each stage of life is marked by certain developmental issues. Developmental crises arise predictably during the college years, and educators can help prepare students to deal with these issues by increasing awareness and skills. Independence, career decision making, developing mature social relationships, and values clarification are major issues that are wrestled with and resolved during the young adult years (Chickering and Reisser, 1993).

In addition, the college social environment presents other issues that can be addressed during orientation. Issues often receiving attention during orientation include safety, wellness, substance abuse, sexual relationships, and personal responsibility. Many of these issues can be confronted by addressing the standards and concerns on matters such as sexual harassment and alcohol and drug use policies. Becoming aware of these personal and social issues can prepare students to learn and deal with lifelong issues more effectively.

Characteristics of Successful Orientation Programs

Successful orientation programs have several characteristics in common that distinguish excellent programs from others that fail to meet their program objectives.

Total Campus Commitment. "The best orientation experience occurs when there is total campus commitment to the process, resulting from collaborative efforts of students, senior administrators, faculty, and the broad spectrum of Student Affairs and educational support programmers" (Smith and Brackin, 1993, p. 35). A spirit of campus cooperation and commitment to student learning and professional development projects a strong sense of the campus as a learning community to incoming students.

Orientation provides faculty and student affairs professionals an opportunity to learn from each other. To be truly effective in orienting new students to the campus environment, student affairs staff and faculty need to understand and appreciate professional roles and issues beyond their own training. Student affairs staff need to be knowledgeable about academic life and faculty issues such as research demands for promotion and tenure, as well as the demands of the adviser role. Faculty need to learn more about student development theory, the role of student affairs offices, and other program issues that are not directly related to classroom teaching and learning. Knowledge, appreciation, and cooperation between student affairs staff and faculty are essential in providing strong collaboration to support new students and their parents. This understanding also provides the basis for building learning communities.

Orientation Activities Prior to Beginning Classes. Orientation programs can be offered at different times in the matriculation process. There appear to be some distinguishing characteristics of these programs in terms of their contributions to student learning. Typical formats include prematriculation and early registration programs, pre-fall programs, and combined designs. Almost all of the institutions surveyed offered some type of prematriculation program, with half requiring participation of all incoming freshmen. These programs vary in length from one day to a full week, with a tendency for smaller institutions to offer longer programs.

Prematriculation and Early Registration Programs. Prematriculation and early registration programs are usually offered in the late spring or early summer prior to college entry. These programs provide new students an opportunity to become more familiar with the college campus and complete placement testing, academic advising, and registration for fall classes. Parent programs are frequently included to help family members learn more about the campus and become important partners in the learning community. Information about student life and campus culture is general and future-oriented, but sets the groundwork for future learning. A variety of sessions are usually offered so that participants get personalized attention. A primary goal is to help participants feel confident about their chosen college or university after the orientation experience.

Pre-Fall Programs. Pre–fall semester programs are held immediately before the start of the fall semester and last from one day to a week. These programs focus on transition to college life for all new students and provide timely, relevant information about the campus culture and expectations of campus community members.

To what extent orientation activities are personalized depends on the size of the campus and freshman class, but there is a general emphasis on making connections among students and community-building activities. Experiential learning activities such as off-campus outings and team building may be offered, especially at smaller institutions. Academic success skills, career planning, and leadership skills are often addressed. These programs offer a good opportunity to begin a more in-depth examination of student life issues such as alcohol use, acquaintance rape, AIDS, and diversity. Behavioral norms and expectations for social and academic conduct may be addressed. Placement testing, academic advising, and registration are also included if there was no prematriculation or early registration program.

Combined Designs. Some campuses offer a combination of programs. The University of Missouri–Rolla offers spring and summer prematriculation and early registration programs for incoming students and their parents, and a campus community orientation for students before the fall semester. Specialized credit-bearing academic courses and a student success course are offered along with orientation activities the week before classes begin. These courses provide exposure to academia without the pressure of the regular semester, thus further enhancing the transition experience.

Spring and summer prematriculation programs generally emphasize academic placement, course registration, and parent programs. Pre–fall semester programs usually tend to emphasize academic success and community integration.

Freshman-Year Orientation Activities. Orientation to the campus does not end when classes begin. The entire freshman year is a critical time to build commitment to higher education, with programs taking the form of orientation courses, academic enhancement services and programs, learning communities, and mentoring. All these efforts help students become fully integrated into the campus community, enhancing the learning process.

Orientation Courses. Many campuses extend their orientation activities into the academic year through semester-long or year-long orientation courses. Some campuses require these courses for all freshmen or special populations, while other campuses make them open electives. These courses are usually taught by faculty and student affairs staff. Their credit status and academic home vary widely.

Our survey indicates that orientation courses focus on campus support services, increasing familiarity with the campus, college transitions, and campus expectations of students. These programs also address academic survival skill training through the discussion of topics like time management, study skills, test anxiety, and career planning. Issues related to personal and social integration, such as social networking, community building, and student development, receive less direct attention. Personal responsibility, wellness, diversity, substance abuse, and issues related to sexual relationships and personal safety are addressed to a moderate degree.

Tusculum College in Greenville, Tennessee, offers a class called Our Lives in Community, which focuses on the personal and social integration of students. Students explore the campus community, self-governance, the civic arts mission of the campus, the students' impact on their community, and the career decision-making process.

Freshman-year courses are sometimes designed to facilitate the transition and academic success of special populations. For example, the University of Idaho offers Transition Seminar—Reentry Connection for Adult Learners to address campus resources and information, career and life planning, coping skills, and study skills. A follow-up of students completing the Transition Seminar indicates a significantly increased retention rate of 82 percent. This figure exceeds general nationwide freshman retention rates and indicates the potential success of this type of course to enhance transitions, learning, and student success.

It has been shown that orientation courses can facilitate academic and social integration, increase student involvement, and enhance the sense of belonging to the campus community. Increased involvement and commitment lead to greater student satisfaction and retention (Astin, 1993; Barefoot and Gardner, 1993; Davis, 1992). These courses increase persistence because their highly interactive, small-group format enables students to obtain support from each other and the instructor (Fidler, 1991). Freshman seminars that achieve maximum student-to-student and student-to-faculty interaction result in higher rates of retention from the freshman to the sophomore year (Barefoot and Gardner, 1993).

Academic Enhancement Services and Programs. Some approaches specifically focus on academic skill development, such as tutoring in specific courses and short courses on study skills, time management, test taking, and career development. Learning centers typically offer test files, peer tutors, and skill enhancement programs and may be located in centralized campus locations and in campus living units. These programs can help students develop strategies to enhance learning and performance in college courses. These services are critical for many new freshmen, who often lack the requisite study skills and personal discipline required to be successful in college.

Learning Communities. Collaborative learning is an approach that combines learning enhancement with community building. Summer bridge programs are sometimes used to provide supplementary academic programs, study groups, and community building prior to the first fall semester. Bridge programs have been shown to increase student success, commitment, and retention. Clustering is also used to build community among new members. Learning communities are deliberately structured clusters of courses that seek to foster communication among students, faculty, advisers, and administrators (Matthews, 1993; Smith, 1991). Students can be grouped together in classes, activities, projects, or living units. One of the most important functions of learning communities is to promote social interactions among peers in and out of class (Tinto, Goodsell Love, and Russo, 1994). The University of Nebraska in Lincoln initiated its Freshman Learning Community in the fall of 1995 by grouping freshmen in living units, an orientation course, and two other courses. Faculty who teach these courses meet students outside class time in their living unit.

Mentoring. Mentoring programs using faculty, staff, and returning students provide new students with personalized relationships to enhance the transition and learning process. "Mentoring in educational institutions can be defined as a one-to-one learning relationship between an experienced person and a younger person that is based on modeling behavior and extended dialogue between them. Mentoring is a way of individualizing a student's education by allowing or encouraging the student to connect with a college staff member who is experienced in a particular field or set of skills" (Lester and Johnson, 1981, p. 50). When mentoring is both formal and informal, students experience the relationship more positively.

There seem to be a variety of interpretations regarding what constitutes mentoring. For example, the University of South Carolina uses peer leaders who serve as mentors to team teach with university faculty and staff. The peer mentors develop leadership skills through their work experiences, training workshops, and enrollment in a credit class called The Teacher as Manager. Peer mentors coteach a course entitled Academic Career Skills and provide informal, out-of-class contact with protégés at Transylvania University in Lexington, Kentucky. The University of Alaska's AHAINA Program uses peer mentors to track students of color during the freshman year. Peer mentors for African American students at West Virginia University's PASSKey program, meet weekly with groups of protégés to address topics such as time management, stress management, and study skills, and they meet individually with protégés twice a semester. Other schools have a variety of contacts with new students that are referred to as mentoring. These contacts may be through student ambassadors, peer educators, resident assistants, student leaders, and campus personnel.

Program Evaluation and Improvement Methods. Ongoing assessment of program effectiveness is important and should include data on participant needs, expectations, experience, satisfaction, and program process evaluation. Individuals can be surveyed prior to program attendance to determine their expectations of the program and perceived needs. Knowledge of participant expectations can be used to design the orientation program.

Standardized instruments, such as the PEEK: Perceptions, Expectations, Emotions, and Knowledge about College (Weinstein, Palmer, and Hanson, 1995), can be used to gain a better idea of incoming students' expectations of college life. Campuses sometimes develop their own local instruments for this purpose and can make them as brief or as detailed as needed. Focus groups, small-group discussions, and other similar methods can be used to obtain the same types of information.

Process evaluations are also important to determine participants' satisfaction with the program and to highlight concerns not being addressed. Almost half of the institutions surveyed assess participant satisfaction with orientation programs. This proportion seems low given the need to understand how well we meet the needs of our primary customers. Satisfaction assessment needs to cover specific components of the orientation program rather than be done as a single global assessment. Most programs involve a number of different activities, and participants' satisfaction with various components will vary. Obtaining only a global rating will not be useful in making programmatic changes that are indicated for specific activities.

These reviews allow all organizing (and implementing) participants to process their experiences and to modify the programs for future use. Internal reviews also allow for formal continuous quality improvement via program evaluations and analyses. Our survey indicates that only a limited number of schools prepare formal program reports for campus distribution. It appears that little in the way of formal continuous improvement activity is occurring to inform possible changes in orientation programs.

Summary: Implications for Student Learning

Orientation programs help students make adjustments to college life and, most important, help them establish the expectations, knowledge, and behaviors that can lead to attainment of academic goals. It is clear that orientation helps many students with both academic learning and learning outside the classroom: personal and professional development are both enhanced by the process. Involvement, a critical factor in success and retention (Astin, 1993), is increased through participation in orientation programs. Students have an opportunity to interact with current students, other incoming students, and with faculty and staff members, thereby creating many valuable connections at the outset of their college experience. Confusion, which many new students experience, is reduced, and their sense of commitment to the campus can be increased.

Orientation provides an opportunity to begin to understand the campus as a social system that is a microcosm of the larger society into which the students will be moving after graduation. An appreciation of the issues that are of concern in the larger society can be enhanced in the orientation process through deliberate attempts to raise awareness levels of new students about these issues. Thus, students' out-of-class learning is enhanced not only in regard to immediate campus issues, but in regard to larger social issues as well. It is obvious that students are positively affected through participation in orientation experiences. Pascarella and Terenzini state, "The weight of evidence does suggest a statistically significant positive link between exposure to various orientation experiences and persistence, both from freshman to sophomore year and from freshman year through attainment of the bachelor's degree" (1991, p. 403).

It is difficult to identify an area of college experience that is not actually or potentially affected during orientation. Clearly, an effective orientation program can do much to facilitate students' transitions into and through college. Conversely, the lack of a quality orientation creates a deficit that may be difficult for many students to overcome (Mullendore and Abraham, 1993).

Each campus community must tailor its orientation programs to the needs of its students. Many different program structures, time frames in which they are offered, and types of program content are evident in the programs surveyed from 273 colleges across the country. These differences indicate that a range of needs are being met with these programs. Significant improvements in orientation programs can be implemented by conducting a thorough assessment of the needs of incoming students and their parents. To the extent that orientation programs are based on such an understanding of participants' needs, it is likely that they are serving a valuable role in enhancing the curricular and cocurricular learning of new students.

References

Astin, A. W. *What Matters in College? Four Critical Years Revisited.* San Francisco: Jossey-Bass, 1993.

Barefoot, B., and Gardner, J. N. "The Freshman Orientation Seminar: Extending the Benefits of Traditional Orientation." In M. L. Upcraft, R. H. Mullendore, B. O. Barefoot, and D. S. Fidler (eds.), *Designing Successful Transitions: A Guide for Orienting Students to College.* Monograph no. 13. Columbia: National Resource Center for the Freshman Year Experience, National Orientation Directors Association, University of South Carolina, 1993.

Chickering, A. W., and Reisser, L. *Education and Identity.* (2nd ed.) San Francisco: Jossey-Bass, 1993.

Council for the Advancement of Standards for Student Service Development Programs. *CAS Standards and Guidelines for Student Support Services/Development Programs.* Washington, D.C.: Council for the Advancement of Standards for Student Service Development Programs, 1986.

Davis, B. "Freshman Seminar: A Broad Spectrum of Effectiveness." *Journal of the Freshman Year Experience,* 1992, 4, 79–94.

Fidler, P. "Relationship of Freshman Orientation Seminars to Sophomore Return Rates." *Journal of the Freshman Year Experience,* 1991, 3, 7–38.

Frost, S. H. *Academic Advising for Student Success: A System of Shared Responsibility.* ASHE-ERIC Higher Education Report, no. 3. Washington, D.C.: Association for the Study of Higher Education, 1991.

Gardner, J., and Hansen, D. "Perspectives on the Future of Orientation." In M. L. Upcraft, R. H. Mullendore, B. O. Barefoot, and D. S. Fidler (eds.), *Designing Successful Transitions: A Guide for Orienting Students to College*. Monograph no. 13. Columbia: National Resource Center for the Freshman Year Experience, National Orientation Directors Association, University of South Carolina, 1993.

Kramer, G. L., and Spencer, R. W. "Academic Advising." In M. L. Upcraft, J. N. Gardner, and Associates, *The Freshman Year Experience: Helping Students Survive and Succeed in College*. San Francisco: Jossey-Bass, 1989.

Lester, V., and Johnson, C. "The Learning Dialogue: Mentoring." In J. Fried (ed.), *Education for Student Development*. New Directions for Student Services, no. 15. San Francisco: Jossey-Bass, 1981.

Matthews, R. "Enriching Teaching and Learning Through Learning Communities." In T. O'Banion (ed.), *Teaching and Learning in the Community College*. Washington, D.C.: American Association of Community Colleges, 1993.

Mullendore, R. H., and Abraham, J. "Organization and Administration of Orientation Programs." In M. L. Upcraft, R. H. Mullendore, B. O. Barefoot, and D. S. Fidler (eds.), *Designing Successful Transitions: A Guide for Orienting Students to College*. Monograph no. 13. Columbia: National Resource Center for the Freshman Year Experience, National Orientation Directors Association, University of South Carolina, 1993.

Noel, L., Levitz, R., Saluri, D., and Associates. *Increasing Student Retention: New Challenges and Potential*. San Francisco: Jossey-Bass, 1985.

Pace, C. R. *College Student Experiences Questionnaire*. (3rd ed.) Bloomington: Indiana University, 1994.

Pascarella, E. T., and Terenzini, P. T. *How College Affects Students: Findings and Insights from Twenty Years of Research*. San Francisco: Jossey-Bass, 1991.

Porter, O. *Undergraduate Completion and Persistence in Four-Year Colleges and Universities*. Washington, D.C.: National Institute of Independent Colleges and Universities, 1990.

Sax, L. J., Astin, A. W., Korn, W. S., and Mahoney, K. M. *The American Freshman: National Norms for Fall 1995*. Los Angeles: Higher Education Research Institute, University of California, 1995.

Schroeder, C. C., Mable, P., and Associates. *Realizing the Educational Potential of Residence Halls*. San Francisco: Jossey-Bass, 1994.

Sheets, C., and Zakely, J. "Academic Transitions and Orientation." Paper presented at the National Orientation Directors Conference, Minneapolis, Minn., Oct. 1995.

Smith, B. L. "Taking Structures Seriously: The Learning Community Model." *Liberal Education*, 1991, 77 (2), 42–48.

Smith, B., and Brackin, R. "Components of a Comprehensive Orientation Program." In M. L. Upcraft, R. H. Mullendore, B. O. Barefoot, and D. S. Fidler (eds.), *Designing Successful Transitions: A Guide for Orienting Students to College*. Monograph no. 13. Columbia: National Resource Center for the Freshman Year Experience, National Orientation Directors Association, University of South Carolina, 1993.

Thomas, R. "Programs and Activities for Improved Retention." In D. Hossler, J. P. Bean, and Associates, *The Strategic Management of College Enrollments*. San Francisco: Jossey-Bass, 1990.

Tinto, V. *Leaving College: Rethinking the Causes and Cures of Student Attrition*. Chicago: University of Chicago Press, 1987.

Tinto, V. *Leaving College: Rethinking the Causes and Cures of Student Attrition*. (2nd ed.) Chicago: University of Chicago Press, 1993.

Tinto, V., Goodsell Love, A., and Russo, P. *Building Learning Communities for New College Students*. University Park, Pa.: National Center on Postsecondary Teaching, Learning, and Assessment, 1994.

Upcraft, M. L., and Gardner, J. N. *The Freshman Year Experience: Helping Students Survive and Succeed in College*. San Francisco: Jossey-Bass, 1989.

Weinstein, C. E., Palmer, D. R., and Hanson, G. R. *PEEK: Perceptions, Expectations, Emotions, and Knowledge About College*. Clearwater, Fla.: H&H, 1995.

White, E. R., Goetz, J. J., Hunter, M. S., and Barefoot, B. O. "Creating Successful Transitions Through Academic Advising." In M. L. Upcraft and G. L. Kramer (eds.), *First-Year Academic Advising: Patterns in the Present, Pathways to the Future*. Monograph no. 18. Columbia: National Resource Center for the Freshman Year Experience and Students in Transition, University of South Carolina, 1995.

Debra A. G. Robinson is director of counseling and career development and coordinator of freshman orientation, University of Missouri–Rolla.

Carl F. Burns is director of academic assessment and assistant director of counseling and career development, University of Missouri–Rolla.

Kevin F. Gaw is test coordinator and counseling psychologist at the Counseling and Career Development Center, University of Missouri–Rolla.

The research related to the impact of residence hall programs on student learning is discussed. Nineteen existing programs focusing on student learning are presented for review.

Strategies for Enhancing Student Learning in Residence Halls

W. Garry Johnson, Kathryn M. Cavins

There has been a renewed interest in the undergraduate experience at colleges and universities in the United States and for that matter around the world. Critics have voiced concern about the undergraduate experience and the impact that it has on student learning. We have seen a renewed interest in and a rejuvenation of the long-ignored undergraduate curriculum at colleges and universities in the United States and around the world. Numerous groups at the local and national level have called for significant reform in all levels of higher education, but particular interest has been focused at the undergraduate level.

The Wingspread report, *An American Imperative: Higher Expectations for Higher Education* (Wingspread Group on Higher Education, 1993), calls for major reform and underscores the notion "that there are at least three fundamental issues common to all 3,400 colleges and universities—taking values seriously; putting student learning first; and creating a nation of learners." Values education and student learning have been topics of interest to housing and residence life professionals for many years. The positive and purposeful impact of the residence hall environment on student learning has been a priority and topic of discussion at national and regional meetings of the Association of College and University Housing Officers–International for most of the last decade.

Educational Potential of Residence Halls

Schroeder, Mable, and Associates (1994, p. 4) make the point that "all efforts to reform higher education have overlooked the educational potential of residence halls." The interactive and pragmatic nature of the residential experience for hundreds of thousands of young people speaks to the need for engagement on the part of students. Pascarella and Terenzini (1991, p. 32), writing about factors contributing to student learning, indicate that "the greatest impact [on their learning] may stem from the students' level of campus engagement, particularly when academic, interpersonal, and extracurricular involvements are mutually supporting and relevant to a particular educational outcome." The vast majority of individuals involved in campus life would argue that residence hall environments, with their rich and diverse student population, are engaging and stimulating for those who live in them. Many parents who visit sons and daughters or listen to their stories during breaks or telephone calls would also confirm the level of involvement and activity provided in the nation's residence halls. In fact, Pascarella, Terenzini, and Blimling (1994, pp. 25–26) state, "Residential living during college is consistently one of the most important determinants of a college student's level of involvement or integration into the various cultural, social, and extracurricular systems of the institution. Compared to their counterparts who live at home or commute to college, resident students have significantly more social interaction with peers and faculty and are more likely to be involved in extracurricular activities and to use campus facilities."

Developing Community

The development of community in our society has long been at the very heart of our nation's values. Gardner (1989, p. 73) notes: "We know that where community exists it confers upon its members identity, a sense of belonging, and a measure of security. . . . Communities are the ground-level generators and preservers of values and ethical systems. The ideals of justice and compassion are nurtured in communities." Building a sense of community on the college campus is not the responsibility of the housing staff alone. Community building must be a commitment embraced by the total institution as part of its core values. In his writings on improving higher education, Boyer (1987, p. 69) notes that "throughout an effective college education, students should become personally empowered and also committed to the common good." Anchors, Douglas, and Kasper (1993, p. 461) point out that, consistent with Boyers's earlier notion, "This empowerment and personal commitment is most likely to occur when student affairs professionals devote thought and energy to creating healthy communities and is a major challenge for contemporary residence hall programs that espouse student development goals." Building community is an important goal for residence hall programs. Anchors, Douglas, and Kasper (1993, p. 462) make the point that "Effective residence halls are not educationally neutral; they create environments and purposive interventions that are designed to enhance the academic experience and personal lives of students."

Research Implications

A rich body of research on the impact of residence halls on students is available for those who wish to explore the subject. Specifically, the literature on campus residence and persistence to graduation, living arrangements and academic achievement, housing assignments by academic ability, and the impact of freshman residence halls on academic achievement speak to the positive relationship between campus living and student success. The current interest in living learning environments and residential colleges and student learning in general will add to the growing fund of knowledge over the next few years.

Campus Residence and Persistence to Graduation. A considerable amount of research exists on the positive relationship between campus residence and rates of persistence and graduation (Anderson, 1981; Astin, 1977, 1982; Pascarella and Chapman, 1983; Tinto, 1987; and Velez, 1985). To further underscore the importance and value of place of residence during college, one need only look to Astin (1977) and the results of his research, which leads him to estimate that living in a residence hall increases a student's likelihood of persistence and graduation by almost 12 percent over students who live elsewhere. Certainly the data presented makes a strong case for the value of the residential experience and underscores the importance of residence halls on the nation's campuses. The data also point to the relative importance of the observation made by Schroeder, Mable, and Associates (1994, p. 4) concerning the potential to be realized using residence halls as an educational forum for college students.

Living Arrangements and Academic Achievement. The issue of living arrangements and academic achievement (grades) has been discussed in the academy for a number of years. Research on both sides of the issue abounds. Studies supporting higher grades have been reported by numerous researchers (May, 1974; Norwack and Hanson, 1985; Simono, Wachowiak, and Furr, 1984). Studies supporting no significant difference in academic achievement based on place of residence have been reported as well (Hunter, 1977; Taylor and Hanson, 1971). Blimling (1989) conducted a metanalysis of the impact of place of residence on grades and concluded that place of residence had no significant influence on academic achievement.

Residence Hall Assignment by Academic Ability. The issue of assigning students to residence halls based on academic ability has been the subject of numerous studies. The weight of the evidence suggests that high-ability students living with other high-ability students do better than those assigned randomly (DeCoster, 1966, 1968; Duncan and Stoner, 1976; Taylor and Hanson, 1971). Pascarella, Terenzini, and Blimling (1994, p. 35) attempt to explain the results by saying, "In short, the residence grouping of high-ability students creates a peer culture in which initial aptitudes and motivation are accentuated and converted into academic accomplishments that are even higher than expected."

Available research suggests that certain types of campus living options may produce different outcomes for college students (Kuh, Schuh, Whitt, and Assoc., 1991; Pascarella and Terenzini, 1991). The majority of evidence seems to suggest positive outcomes on measures of social climate, academic performance, and persistence (Centra, 1968; Clark and others, 1988; Felver, 1983; Pascarella and Terenzini, 1980, 1981).

Freshman Residence Halls and Academic Achievement. The impact of freshman residence halls on academic achievement is mixed according to the available evidence. Positive relationships have been reported (Ballou, 1986; Cheslin, 1967), whereas negative relationships were reported by Schoemer and McConnell (1970). There has been a significant amount of work done recently with the development of first-year experience programs, made popular by John Gardner and the staff of the National Research Center for the Freshman Year Experience, at the University of South Carolina. Zeller, Fidler, and Barefoot (1991) present a number of recommendations or goals for the first-year experience. Numerous institutions have used these goals in developing their own programs for first-year students. The National Center for the Freshman Year Experience currently conducts workshops and conferences worldwide on issues relating to the impact of the initial year of college on students. National and regional professional conferences offer numerous opportunities to learn more about what institutions are doing to enhance students' introduction to the collegiate experience.

The impact of first-year experience programs has been studied by a number of researchers and, with few exceptions (Banzinger, 1986; Wilkie and Kuckuch, 1989), the results suggest a significant relationship between various orientation experiences and college persistence from freshman to sophomore year and on to graduation (Bron and Gordon, 1986; Farr, Jones, and Samprone, 1986; Fidler and Hunter, 1989). Pascarella and Terenzini (1991, p. 403) point out that "the most consistently effective program format appears to be a first-semester freshman seminar that meets as a regular class with an assigned instructor." Many institutions nationwide are adopting first-year programs that meet in residence halls and involve faculty and student affairs professionals in a team teaching role. New programs often involve the class as part of the living and learning experience throughout the first year of college, not just during the first semester.

Summary of Research Findings

The evidence on balance indicates that residence halls have a positive impact on students in a number of important areas, including grades, persistence, satisfaction with the institution, psychosocial development, self-esteem, critical thinking, involvement in extracurricular activities, and graduation. Given the positive impact of the residential experience as outlined here and the current state of higher education in the United States, the observation made by Schroeder, Mable, and Associates (1994, p. 4) is most appropriate. They state, "As colleges and universities across the country are being challenged by economic agendas, shifting demographics, increasingly diverse student populations, public demand for quality and accountability, and faculty concerns about the widening gap between ideal academic standards and actual student learning, residence halls have an opportunity to shape the transformation of higher education."

The issue of how housing and residence life professionals will respond to the challenges presented as a result of the focus on student learning remains to be seen. Schroeder (1995, p. 5) states, "The main challenge for housing programs is the development of clear and coherent educational purposes directly tied to the institution's primary mission—student learning. Clearly delineating learning outcomes and clarifying staff roles and responsibilities for achieving them are elements central to designing educationally purposeful activities."

Faculty Involvement Programs

Carson-Newman College, Laboratory for Learning. In each of the five residence halls on the campus of Carson-Newman College, a residential team comprising faculty, students, and staff was created. Their goals were to plan intensive programming designed to focus student attention on issues related to campus life and academics, and to build a cohesive community between departments, students, faculty, and staff.

The setting encompasses the classroom, residence halls, and cocurricular environments. Students are challenged to attend presentations of faculty, lead and engage in topics of debate, and participate in field trips exploring such topics as multiculturalism, gender issues, and life transition.

Through the Laboratory for Learning, students are learning to connect what they learn in the classroom with human relationships and personal identity, social responsibility, and individuality.

Indiana University, Allies/Fellows/Friends Program. The Allies/Fellows/Friends Program presents residence hall students with an opportunity to interact informally with members of the Indiana University faculty, staff, or community. Allies/Fellows/Friends are paired with a floor and participate in dinner gatherings, programs, and individual consultation.

Allies/Fellows/Friends and students are encouraged to discuss areas of mutual interest: academic, vocational, and cocurricular. By extending the university's academic mission into the residence halls, students realize academic success with the support of a caring university community.

Students who participate in this program perform better academically and are more interested in their course work than those who don't, and grow to appreciate faculty and other adults as partners in their success.

First-Year Experience Programs

University of California at Davis, Residential Education Program. The Residential Education Program is a compilation of support services for first-year students in the residence halls. Most students leave the residence halls after the first year, so this program is geared toward front-loading campus resources. Learning Centers, including computer laboratories, test files, and tutorial sessions are offered in every residential area. Resident advisers are specially trained to address student concerns and help them navigate the university. Residential programming is aimed at teaching students to make connections at the university so that they may successfully solve their problems after they leave the residence halls. On-site academic advising is also provided to the students living in the halls.

University of California–Davis has realized remarkably high retention rates. It is believed that providing support at the early stages of education on this campus assists in the notable graduation rates.

University of Central Arkansas, Residential Instructional Program (RIP). RIP is a supplemental instruction program offered to first-year residence hall students. Upper division students who have demonstrated academic success are recruited to live in one of two first-year halls and serve as tutors for core freshman courses.

RIP leaders tutor one-on-one and facilitate informal seminars in which students compare notes, discuss readings, develop organizational tools, and predict test items. Students are taught how to integrate course content and reasoning skills.

This program is supervised by the undergraduate studies office and is supported by the Department of Housing.

University of Pittsburgh at Johnstown, First-Year Commuting Student Program. The University of Pittsburgh at Johnstown focuses resources on first-year students so they successfully assimilate into the collegiate culture. All first-year students are assigned to a first-year community. Commuting students check into a residence hall room with a locker, study desk, and study amenities as residential students check into their rooms. The commuting students participate in orientation and educational programs, residential governance, and are afforded the same services as residential students. All first-year students have a PAL (peer assistance leader) and an ESP (employee-student partner) who work to link them with important campus resources.

Residence hall staff recognize that learning extends beyond the classroom and take responsibility in creating inclusive environments, supportive of the academic goals of all students.

Western Illinois University, First Year Experience Program. The First Year Experience (FYE) program is a residential program designed to support the academic and personal transitions of new students. Those living in FYE communities participate in a structured fifteen-week program focusing on study skills, relationships, campus resources, money management, and goal setting.

The students are assisted by a resident assistant and peer adviser specifically trained to facilitate first-year success. A faculty mentor acts as an informal adviser, programmer, and friend to each community.

Women living in FYE communities have earned better grade point averages than their counterparts, and both men and women in the FYE program have shown better rates of retention than those living in standard communities.

University of Washington, Freshmen Interest Groups. Freshmen Interest Groups, better known as FIGs, are designed to help make the university seem a bit smaller to new students. A FIG is composed of twenty to twenty-four freshmen with similar interests who enroll in the same cluster of classes during their first quarter on campus. FIG students also come together in a weekly seminar led by a junior or senior student. The seminar provides an opportunity for first-time students to learn about campus resources, discuss time management, meet with faculty in an informal setting, and arrange social activities that build a sense of belonging and community within the group.

Students may choose from between fifty and sixty FIG sections ranging from the arts to the environment to business. Several technology-oriented FIGs involve extensive computer use. In these innovative clusters, students and instructors use laptop computers for collaboration, communication, and class presentations.

Courses are predetermined for each FIG section; by enrolling in the FIG, a student is automatically enrolled in a specific set of courses. Detailed information on FIG sections is available during New Student Orientation and students can sign up at that time. For example, one FIG is titled Knowing Our Universe; it involves four classes that all students who enroll in it take: Introduction to Astronomy; Introduction to the History of Science; Composition: Literature; and a common orientation class called University Resources, Information, and Technology. A FIG titled Culture and Gender requires that the students take Introduction to Anthropology; Introduction to Women's Studies; Composition: Social Issues; and the University Resources, Information, and Technology class.

Theme Housing Programs

University of Louisville, Living Learning Communities. To promote learning outside the classroom, the University of Louisville offers communities based on the lifestyle interests of its students. In building these communities, the housing staff collaborates with faculty, academic support offices, and staff to identify learning opportunities through participation in these communities.

An International House is designed to promote intercultural exchange among students, exposing them to different values, cultures, and traditions. Collaboration with the International Center, Women's Center, and the Multicultural Center supports services and opportunities for students.

The Wellness House was created to promote the development of and teach the skills for a healthy lifestyle. In working with the Health Promotions faculty and the Counseling Center staff, students are given a lifestyle assessment and then map their goals for incorporating wellness with academics.

University of Michigan, 21st Century Program. The 21st Century Program provides an academic experience for leaders of the next century. It provides unique educational experiences in a supportive residential setting. Up to 265 students participate in a weekly seminar to explore personal, university, community, and world issues. Students also meet for Subject Mastery Workshops in which collaborative learning is emphasized. A supportive community is intentionally selected to help students learn in a diverse, friendly, cooperative environment, instead of a random grouping of students.

University of Michigan, WISE: Women in Science and Engineering. In an effort to support and retain an underrepresented population in the science and engineering fields, the University of Michigan designed a lifestyle community in which women can support one another in their academic and career pursuits. The program seeks to connect undergraduate women with other students, faculty, and professionals sharing their interests. Educational and social programs are designed to build skill, form partnerships, and prepare women for a field dominated by men.

WISE students are encouraged to participate in study groups, become involved in an undergraduate research project, and register for WISE course offerings.

University of Nevada, REBEL Leadership Development Series. The REBEL Series is a six-week leadership training course for residence hall students. With *The Seven Habits of Highly Effective People* (Covey, 1989) serving as the text, students are challenged to consider the congruence between their values, life goals, and academic plans.

The focus of the program is self-understanding and exploration of style, talent, and skills. Personal commitment, integrity, and critical thinking are emphasized in all parts of the course.

Evaluation of student learning and motivation is done each week through a free response format. Course offerings fill quickly as a result of past participant recommendation.

Residential College Programs

University of Michigan, Residential College. The Residential College at the University of Michigan is a four-year degree-granting program in the College of Literature, Science and Art. All the classrooms, faculty offices, studios, and administrative offices are located in the building in which students live. Residential College courses are small and engaging, encouraging students to develop special interests while providing a liberal arts base.

Students living in the Residential College are urged to participate in self-governance, provide input to the Educational Policy committee, and air their views at monthly town meetings. They can join fellow students and faculty at theatrical performances, coffee houses, and the library without leaving the residential area.

This program combines the benefits of the small college with the rich culture of a large university.

Michigan State University, Lyman-Briggs School. Approximately nine hundred students participate in this residential college program, which is housed in Holmes Hall and emphasizes science education. Students are admitted into the program on a first-come, first-served bases. There are common general education courses during freshman and sophomore years. Students then choose an area of specialization. Classes, faculty offices, laboratories, housing, food service, and recreational facilities are available in Holmes Hall.

Residence life educators play a unique role in Lyman-Briggs. Two full-time staff members have integrated functions in both student and academic affairs. Both staff members supervise resident assistants and also have academic advising responsibilities. The small size of the school allows for a greater degree of informal faculty involvement in students' lives. On Thursdays, a table is set aside in the cafeteria for a student-faculty-staff lunch. Faculty and residence life staff work together with students on a cocurricular committee, which sponsors a number of activities. Residence life staff advise all student organizations in the college. Faculty and residence life staff jointly present orientation programs. Residence life staff have also provided diversity training for undergraduate teaching assistants.

Michigan State University, James Madison College. The school is housed in the Case residence hall and focuses on interdisciplinary programs in the social sciences. Four major concentration areas are offered, all placing a strong emphasis on developing students' reasoning skills and verbal skills. These areas include International Relations, Political Economy, Political Theory and Constitutional Democracy, and Social Relations. Classrooms, faculty and administrative offices, student housing, food service, and recreation areas are housed in Case Hall.

The residence life program is directed by a full-time staff member. The theme, Academic and Social Excellence, provides an anchor for all residence life activities. A number of programming efforts have a direct link to classroom experiences. During Diversity Week, a program on male-female relationships corresponds to material presented the same day on gender and power in a freshman public affairs course. Faculty have also played a role as guest presenters and speakers in residence life sponsored programming.

University of Miami, Residential College System. In a desire to enhance its reputation as a distinguished private institution, the leadership of the University of Miami worked to develop a residential college system. The initial goals of the system were to provide opportunities to develop intellectual skills that would help students succeed in the classroom, expose students to major disciplines and perspectives outside the classroom, develop a sense of community among undergraduates, expand opportunities for faculty-student interaction, and help new students bond to the university.

Each residential college comprises 400–750 undergraduate students who live in a defined community. They are equipped with full-service computer labs, study lounges, classrooms, conference rooms, and a guest suite for visiting scholars, artists, and dignitaries. Each college is directed by a live-in master, a senior faculty member whose principal responsibility is to set the tone for the college and to work with the residential team to plan programs and activities that enhance the living environment. Other faculty and staff work with the master to provide academic, social, cultural, and recreational programs and to respond to the daily needs and concerns of the community.

University of Missouri–St. Louis, Pierre Laclede Honors College. The Pierre Laclede Honors College is the only honors college in the United States with its own comprehensive, residential campus. Named for the founder of St. Louis and located on a historic estate, the Honors College shares the form and functions of the famous residential colleges of Oxford and Cambridge.

All Honors classes are held in Laclede Hall, an imposing old building of stone, brick, and oak situated on five acres of beautiful lawns and woods. The former convent provides some ten thousand square feet of space for academic purposes, including classrooms, seminar rooms, tutorial rooms, and a computer lab.

Sixty students live in the attached Chouteau Hall, in a single-room environment. The building is co-ed by alternate floor. The college also includes a reference library with over six hundred volumes of reference material for student and faculty use.

Living Learning Centers

University of Michigan, Pilot Program. The Pilot Program is a living-learning community that connects academics with cocurricular interests. Courses are taught in-residence by faculty who live in the halls. Cocurricular activities are closely tied to the learning impact on the participants.

The Pilot Program has been noted for its strong multicultural focus. Integrated in both the academic and social settings of this community, students embrace diversity and employ the skills to live in a multicultural world.

University of Wisconsin–Madison, Bradley Learning Community. Bradley Hall is co-ed by wing and houses 244 first-year students. Assignments to Bradley Hall are based on date of application. Professional staff supervise seven upperclass peer learning partners who help students with transition issues. A student multicultural resident consultant helps the diverse population adjust to campus. A number of faculty fellows join the residence life staff in supporting the students living in Bradley Hall.

Ten faculty fellows from the College of Letters and Science are members of the Bradley Learning Community and have offices on the first floor of the building. Faculty members are all senior faculty.

Students who live in the Bradley Learning Community can earn an interdisciplinary certificate in Integrated Liberal Studies, Global Cultures, or Environmental Studies.

Indiana University, Collins Living Learning Center. The Collins Living Learning Center goal is to promote active learning on the part of students and to bring the learning process into their environment every day. Active learning is promoted through a variety of student-generated programs, which include developing and implementing new courses and publishing a weekly newspaper, a literary magazine, and a yearbook. Students perform plays and are involved in improvisations on the stage of the Cheshire Cafe in the hall. Students take trips to museums and theaters and attend concerts. Students have available to them labs for photography, ceramics, and computers.

The Collins Living Learning Center was founded in 1972 and houses 450 residents. During its tenure, it has featured many outstanding and innovative courses as well as being the scene of many forums and literary, musical, and theatrical events. The center has also played host to many distinguished artists, writers, and public figures.

Summary

Existing research in the field demonstrates that residence halls have a positive impact on students and contribute to the positive feelings they have about the collegiate experience. The data on special living arrangements indicate that intentional academic focus aids in retention and supports academic achievement on the part of residents who take advantage of special lifestyle options. Numerous institutions have developed special living arrangements that have as their core a strong academic focus. A number of the programs featured in this chapter involve topical interest groups, with students living together in a common environment. Many of the programs involve students living together and taking common academic classes, generally in the residence hall environment. A number of the programs involve very active faculty-student contact in both a formal class setting and in the informal residence hall environment itself.

The responses to changing conditions in higher education and the renewed interest in the quality of the undergraduate experience will expand the partnership between student affairs and academic affairs. Contributions to student learning made by student affairs, especially residence halls, will be the subject of considerable discussion during the remainder of the 1990s. Faculty members and student affairs staff will enter into new joint programs designed to improve student learning opportunities and increase the retention rates of students. Residence halls will move beyond the long-outdated scope of dorms in the new reality of the nation's campuses.

Most important in the student learning movement will be the expansion of existing residential programs currently being offered and the development of new and creative programs designed to improve the academic environment on campus. The development of an increasing number of collaborative programs between academic affairs and student affairs will serve as models for other campus partnerships that will focus on enriching the undergraduate experience.

The further development and growth of the student learning initiative will have as its underpinning a number of the programs that have been featured in this chapter. The programs that have been presented relating to faculty involvement, first-year experience, theme housing, freshman interest groups, residential colleges and living learning centers are all programs that can be used as models for other campuses. The programs featured in this chapter must be carefully modified to meet the needs of each specific campus and its students. Much of the groundwork has been done in terms of the organization, role, and impact of these types of programs.

Exciting times are ahead for staff members and faculty who become involved in the movement to improve student learning on campus. Residence halls have the potential to contribute to student success and become the focus of key institutional initiatives designed to improve learning environments and opportunities for undergraduate students. Residence hall staff who embrace the student learning challenge may well be inventing a future for residence halls that most could only imagine a few short years ago.

References

Anchors, S., Douglas, B. D., and Kasper, M. K. "Developing and Enhancing Student Communities." In R. B. Winston, Jr., S. Anchors, and Associates, *Student Housing and Residential Life: A Handbook for Professionals Committed to Student Development Goals.* San Francisco: Jossey-Bass, 1993.

Anderson, K. "Post–High School Experiences and College Attrition." *Sociology of Education,* 1981, *54,* 20.

Astin, A. W. *Four Critical Years: Effects of College on Beliefs, Attitudes, and Knowledge.* San Francisco: Jossey-Bass, 1977.

Astin, A. W. *Minorities in American Higher Education: Recent Trends, Current Prospects, and Recommendations.* San Francisco: Jossey-Bass, 1982.

Ballou, R. "Freshmen in College Residence Halls: A Study of Freshmen Perceptions of Residence Hall Social Climates at Ten Colleges and Universities." *Journal of College and University Student Housing,* 1986, *16,* 7–12.

Banzinger, G. *Evaluating the Freshman Seminar Course and Developing a Model of Intervention with Freshmen.* Unpublished manuscript, Merietta College, Merietta, Ohio, 1986.

Blimling, G. "Meta-Analysis of the Influence of College Residence Halls in Academic Performance." *Journal of College Student Development,* 1989, *30,* 298–308.

Boyer, E. L. *The Undergraduate Experience in America.* New York: HarperCollins, 1987.

Bron, G., and Gordon, M. "Impact of an Orientation Center on Grade Point Average and Attrition." *College Student Journal,* 1986, *20,* 242–246.

Centra, J. "Student Perceptions of Residence Hall Environments: Living Learning vs. Conventional Units." *Journal of College Student Personnel,* 1968, *9,* 266–272.

Cheslin, S. "The Differential Effects of Housing on College Freshmen." Unpublished doctoral dissertation, Department of Education, Michigan State University. *Dissertation Abstracts International,* 1967, *28,* 1675A.

Clarke, J., Misev, K., and Roberts, A. "Freshmen Residential Programs: Effects of Living-Learning Structure, Faculty Involvement, and Thematic Focus." *Journal of College and University Student Housing,* 1988, *18,* 7–13.

Covey, S. R. *The Seven Habits of Highly Effective People.* New York: Simon & Schuster, 1989.

DeCoster, D. "Housing Assignments for High Ability Students." *Journal of College Student Personnel,* 1966, *7,* 147–150.

DeCoster, D. "Effects of Homogeneous Housing Assignments for High Ability Students." *Journal of College Student Personnel*, 1968, *2*, 75–78.

Duncan, C., and Stoner, K. "The Academic Achievement of Residents in a Scholar Residence Hall." *Journal of College and University Student Housing*, 1976, *6*, 7–9.

Farr, W., Jones, J., and Samprone, J. *The Consequences of a College Preparatory and Individual Self-Evaluation Program on Student Achievement and Retention.* Unpublished manuscript, Georgia College, 1986.

Felver, J. A. "Longitudinal Study of the Effects of Living/Learning Programs." Unpublished doctoral dissertation, Northern Illinois University. *Dissertation Abstracts International*, 1983, *44* (12), 3607A.

Fidler, P., and Hunter, M. "How Seminars Enhance Student Success." In M. L. Upcraft, J. N. Gardner, and Associates, *The Freshman Year Experience: Helping Students Survive and Succeed in College.* San Francisco: Jossey-Bass, 1989.

Gardner, J. W. "Building Community." *Kettering Review*, 1989, *7*, 73–81.

Hunter, J. A. "Comparison of the Academic Achievement of Sophomores Living in University Residence Halls with That of Sophomores Living Off-Campus in Selected State Universities in North Carolina." Unpublished doctoral dissertation, Department of Education, Duke University. *Dissertation Abstracts International*, 1977, *38* (8), 4604A.

Kuh, G., Schuh, J., Whitt, E., and Associates. *Involving Colleges: Successful Approaches to Fostering Student Learning and Development Outside the Classroom.* San Francisco: Jossey-Bass, 1991.

May, E. "Type of Housing and Achievement of Disadvantaged University Students." *College Student Journal*, 1974, *8*, 48–51.

Norwack, K., and Hanson, A. "Academic Achievement of Freshmen as a Function of Residence Hall Housing." *NASPA Journal*, 1985, *22*, 22–28.

Pascarella, E., and Chapman, D. "Validation of a Theoretical Model of College Withdrawal: Interaction Effects in a Multi-Institutional Sample." *Research in Higher Education*, 1983, *19*, 25–48.

Pascarella, E., and Terenzini, P. "Student-Faculty and Student-Peer Relationships as Mediators of the Structural Effects of Undergraduate Residence Arrangement." *Journal of Educational Research*, 1980, *73*, 344–353.

Pascarella, E., and Terenzini, P. "Residence Arrangement, Student-Faculty Relationships, and Freshman-Year Educational Outcomes." *Journal of College Student Personnel*, 1981, *22*, 147–156.

Pascarella, E. T., and Terenzini, P. T. *How College Affects Students: Findings and Insights from Twenty Years of Research.* San Francisco: Jossey-Bass, 1991.

Pascarella, E. T., Terenzini, P. T., and Blimling, G. "The Impact of Residence Life on Students." In C. C. Schroeder, P. Mable, and Associates, *Realizing the Educational Potential of Residence Halls.* San Francisco: Jossey-Bass, 1994.

Schoemer, J., and McConnell, W. "Is There a Case for the Freshmen Women's Residence Hall?" *Personnel and Guidance Journal*, 1970, *49*, 35–40.

Schroeder, C. C. "Student Learning: An Imperative for Housing Programs Committed to Educating Students." Association of College and University Housing Officers–International, *Talking Stick*, 1995, *13*, 4–7.

Schroeder, C. C., Mable, P., and Associates, *Realizing the Educational Potential of Residence Halls.* San Francisco: Jossey-Bass, 1994.

Simono, R., Wachowiak, D., and Furr, S. "Student Living Environments and Their Perceived Impact on Academic Performance: A Brief Follow-Up." *Journal of College and University Student Housing*, 1984, *10*, 26–28.

Taylor, R., and Hanson, G. "Environmental Impact on Achievement and Study Habits." *Journal of College Student Personnel*, 1971, *12*, 445–454.

Tinto, V. *Leaving College: Rethinking the Causes and Cures of Student Attrition.* Chicago: University of Chicago Press, 1987.

Velez, W. "Finishing College: The Effects of College Type." *Sociology of Education*, 1985, *58*, 191–200.

Wilkie, C., and Kuckuck, S. "A Longitudinal Study of the Effects of a Freshman Seminar." *Journal of the Freshman Year Experience*, 1989, *1*, 7–16.

Wingspread Group on Higher Education. *An American Imperative: Higher Expectations for Higher Education*. Racine, Wis.: Wingspread Group on Higher Education, Johnson Foundation, 1993.

Zeller, W., Fidler, D., and Barefoot, B. (eds.). *Residence Life Programs and the First Year Experience*, Columbia, S.C.: Association of College and University Housing Officers–International/National Resource Center for the Freshman Year Experience, 1991.

W. GARRY JOHNSON is associate vice president for student services and associate professor of counselor education and college student personnel at Western Illinois University, Macomb, Illinois.

KATHRYN M. CAVINS is associate director of residence life at Western Illinois University, Macomb, Illinois.

Academic courses taught by student affairs staff are described in this chapter. Specific emphasis is placed on the learning outcomes for such activities.

Academic Courses Offered by Student Affairs: A Sampler

John H. Schuh

The content of contemporary courses offered by student affairs staff has long been a part of the landscape of higher education. Orientation courses for freshmen, for example, can be identified as early as 1888, according to Dwyer (1989). The syllabi of these courses "ranged widely" (p. 37), but included such topics as how to study, citizenship, career counseling, and the unique problems faced by special populations of students. From this modest beginning, courses offered by student affairs professionals have become more widespread to the point where such courses are common on contemporary college campuses.

This chapter describes and discusses courses offered by student affairs staff, but it does not address courses offered by student affairs practitioners as part of student affairs preparation programs, or similar programs used to prepare counselors, counseling psychologists, and the like. The primary, although not exclusive, focus is on undergraduate courses rather than courses offered as part of graduate preparation programs.

The Internet was used to obtain the syllabi identified in this chapter. An announcement was posted through several discussion groups, asking colleagues to submit the syllabi for courses they offered. Without electronic mail, this process might have been much more cumbersome, and would have required a mass mailing or telephone campaign. The process worked quite well. A wide variety of course materials was submitted. These materials provided substantial information upon which much of this chapter is based. The reader should understand that no claim is made that the courses discussed in this chapter represent the universe of such courses. It is highly probable that many other courses are available on other college campuses.

NEW DIRECTIONS FOR STUDENT SERVICES, no. 75, Fall 1996 © Jossey-Bass Publishers

Historical Perspective

The literature that describes academic courses offered by student affairs staff is not particularly robust. Orientation courses, however, have been described by several authors. As Gordon (1989) points out, orientation courses were begun at Boston University in 1888 and proliferated in the years before World War I. "Most incorporated topics designed to inform the student about their institution and the various aspects of college life in general" (p. 185).

A contemporary orientation course, in the view of Jewler (1989), would include academic, vocational, social, physical, emotional, and spiritual topics in addition to library research methods, career and academic major planning, writing experiences, and the use of textbooks or other appropriate reading materials. As Jewler observes, "No two individuals teach University 101 in quite the same manner" (p. 201). One variation on this theme is reported by Denson (1994), who describes a freshman seminar that addresses the unique needs of intercollegiate athletes.

A second area where courses have a historical presence is that of resident assistant training. Winston and Fitch (1993) advocate the development of a training course that prospective resident assistants complete before being selected for their positions. Citing the research of Winston and Buckner, they conclude that taking such a course prior to the work experience can reduce job stress and raise staff effectiveness. They recommend that such a training course focus primarily on helping skills and be open to all students on campus, and should be taught over thirty-five to forty contact hours. It should include such topic areas as basic helping skills, values clarification activities, knowledge of cultural differences, basic group dynamics and group leadership, student development theories, crisis intervention, providing accurate information, making effective referrals, and dealing with difficult circumstances. They recommend that successful completion of this type of course at a grade level of B be a prerequisite for selection as a resident assistant (Winston and Fitch, 1993).

Another approach to academic course work is the Education of Self course, which is described by Lenton and Duvall (1980). This course is designed to "develop within the individual a sense of self-worth and the value of people and life itself" (p. 170). The course includes such elements as readings, awareness experiences, a weekend workshop, and learning reports. Within this course, the student is "challenged to gain the attitudes, information, and skills necessary for systematic lifelong learning to increase one's ability to develop continuing personal strategies necessary for living in a complex world" (p. 169).

Ender and Carranza (1991) present a model training course for study skills paraprofessionals and tutors. The goals of the course include students' understanding their role as paraprofessional helper, understanding the influence of paraprofessionals on other students' cognitive and psychosocial development, learning to assist others on a one-to-one basis, modeling college study skills and assisting others in the development of those skills, demonstrating referral strategies and understanding the purpose of various resources, and demonstrating skills and competencies necessary to provide appropriate interventions in the assigned areas (p. 548). Students are evaluated through class attendance and participation, reading assigned materials, and completing a number of written projects. This three-credit course is a mandatory requirement for those who wish to apply for the paraprofessional study skills assistant and tutor position on the authors' campus.

Habley (1984) describes an approach whereby course credit is awarded to academic advisers at the University of Montana for their participation in training and service activities. They participate in fourteen hours of preservice training and meet at least once per month for two hours to discuss their paraprofessional activities. In turn, the students receive one quarter hour of credit for each thirty hours of service to the program. Students, according to this report, earn three or four quarter hours of credit over the course of the year.

Several other courses have been described in recent literature. Hardy and Karathanos (1992) describe a bridge course to prepare at-risk students for regular university courses. This course was offered by professional advising staff on their campus. A collaborative effort for freshman engineering students was reported by Robinson (1994). This course involved counseling and career exploration staff working with engineering faculty to help students prepare for the engineering curriculum.

A recent study of 563 institutions conducted by Ender, Newton, and Caple (1996) revealed that student affairs professional staff hold faculty rank at 53 percent of the responding institutions. Formal courses taught by student affairs staff were offered by 62 percent of the institutions surveyed.

Course Syllabi

An examination of the syllabi for the courses submitted yielded several common characteristics for each course. These included course goals and objectives, instructional techniques, course materials, and various evaluation strategies.

Goals and Course Objectives. As one might imagine, the goals of these courses vary widely. Nonetheless, it is possible to classify the courses into three groups. Some of the courses are designed to train paraprofessionals, such as resident assistants or other peer helpers. Another set of courses is designed to help students adjust to the challenges of college life in both an academic and social sense. A third group of courses provides opportunities for students to develop specific skills, such as leadership or health and wellness. Although stating the goals and objectives in this fashion makes them seem more separate than they actually are in practice, the taxonomy works well in analyzing the goals of these types of courses. Brief synopses of the goals of these courses follow with a reference for whom the course is designed.

Paraprofessional Training Courses. Introduction to Health Education, offered at the University of Montana, is designed to educate students in the areas of wellness, healthy choices, and risk reduction to prepare them for the practicum experience as a peer health educator (Green, 1995). It has two goals: to provide students with information to help them evaluate their personal wellness and make responsible life choices, and to give students the knowledge and skills necessary to develop and implement health promotion and risk reduction projects for their peers. No mention was made in the syllabus that the course is offered for specific classes of students.

Peer Interventions in Diversity Awareness. This course, offered at the University of Georgia, has six desired learning outcomes. Among them are exposure to the basic concepts and related issues of oppression theory, assessing level of comfort and awareness in relation to issues of differences and multiculturalism, receiving the tools to develop and present programs on diversity and multiculturalism to peers, and being better equipped to live successfully in a culturally changing and diverse society (Porter, Faulkner, and Wall, 1994).

Guidance in School Settings is taught at Indiana University of Pennsylvania (IUP) for paraprofessionals. Its general purpose is to focus on the role and function of undergraduate students serving as paraprofessional helpers with the higher education environment (Ender, 1995a). The goals for the course include to understand their roles as paraprofessional helpers, to understand the impact of paraprofessionals on other students' cognitive and psychosocial development, to be able to assist others through one-to-one contact, and to be able to demonstrate appropriate referral strategies.

As was mentioned earlier, courses that provide training for resident assistants have been common on college campuses for many years. At Wake Forest, such a course is offered to provide for the continuing education and training of new resident assistants that augments their Fall training program and provides important skills and knowledge that enable the resident assistants to better perform important responsibilities of their position (Dunton, 1995). The course also allows for mutual support, enhances unity within the staff, and provides a forum for resident assistants to discuss pertinent issues related to their position.

Peer Sexuality is another example of a training course. It is offered at the University of Georgia (Varley, 1995) and is designed to train peer sexuality educators. Among its objectives are that students will be able to: demonstrate effective group presentation skills; develop and deliver a presentation of their choice on either wellness, drug and alcohol abuse, or sexual assault awareness; be knowledgeable regarding sexually transmitted diseases; discuss the characteristics of healthy and unhealthy relationships; and discuss campus resources for survivors of sexual assault.

Orientation Courses. General Studies 250: University Seminar, offered at San Diego State, is available to first-year students. It is described as providing a unique opportunity for first-time freshmen to meet in small groups to discuss concerns and issues that are important to their success at the university.

Improving academic skills, communicating and using resources available on campus, and tapping into the intellectual life of the campus are elements of the course description (Holmes, 1994). Such courses "serve the function of developing an openness to the college experience while cultivating awareness of what professors do in their disciplines" (Davis, 1995, p. 164).

The Returning Adult Seminar (Ryan and Ladwig, 1995) is designed to ease the transition to Wichita State University for adult students who have been out of higher education for at least a year. Among the topics it covers are connecting to other adult students and university resources, time and stress management, educational and career planning, goal setting, and becoming familiar with the library and computer resources of the university.

A course with similar objectives is offered for new students at Arizona State University. This course is offered through academic services but has been taught by a number of student affairs staff at the university (Henderson, 1995). The general objective for the course is to provide a forum for the development of strategies, skills, and techniques that promote success in higher education.

Skill Development Courses. Career Development for the College Student (Holleran and Hartzell, 1995) is offered at Hartwick College for students as they begin their college careers. The course has five objectives: to understand the basic components of the career development process, to become familiar with the facilities and resources of the college, to develop a career action plan, to develop the tools necessary to implement a job search, and to provide students with an experience with professionals in various career fields.

Comedy, Creativity and Communication is designed to provide information regarding the professional person's use of humor and is available at the University of Montana (Weldon, 1995). Its objectives include the following: to provide students with an interview of current research on humor and its application to wellness and communication; to encourage students to explore, use, and share humor as an interrelated part of a professional setting; to promote creativity and development of humor as one part of the education and helping process; and to become more comfortable with humor in personal life.

Issues in Leadership, offered at Stanford University (Porteus, Howe, and Jackson, 1995), is available to undergraduate students primarily, although master's level students are accepted in limited numbers. Its five objectives are to allow students to explore basic theories and concepts of leadership and personal values, to identify personal leadership styles and skills and to learn how to adapt and use them effectively, to improve and expand their range of leadership skills, to develop a personal approach at Stanford and in the future by integrating personal leadership style and experiences with leadership theory, and to explore cultural differences.

A similar course, Introduction to Leadership Development, is offered at the University of California, Santa Barbara. The primary purpose of this course is to provide an overview of theoretical constructs and practical applications to leadership. The course is designed to assist students in developing individual approaches to effective leadership (Johnson and Buford, 1995).

Wake Forest University offers a related course, Studies in Contemporary Leadership (Gerardy and Ford, 1995). This course provides students with a historical survey of leadership theory, promotes an in-depth understanding of contemporary leadership theory in its various applications in society, requires students to become actively engaged in practical leadership exercises, and has students develop their own philosophy of leadership.

Advising Student Organizations (Dunkel, 1995) is designed for graduate students learning to advise student organizations at the University of Florida. It has four goals for its participants: to increase their knowledge of the nature of the role of a student organization adviser, to increase their knowledge of group development concepts, to expose them to different organizational cultures, and to help them learn to apply their findings to public and private organizations (Dunkel, 1995). The course could also be identified as a paraprofessional training course in that many of these students work with organizations on campus.

Contemporary Social/Health Issues and Peer Programming in Higher Education, offered at the University of Hawaii at Manoa, is designed to explore health and social issues including alcohol and drug use, HIV and AIDS, and sexual assault that affect college students and college success. It also provides for the training of peer educators (Willinger, Hansell, and Scholly, 1995).

Alcohol Studies is taught at Oregon State University for undergraduate and graduate students twice each year. Among its eleven objectives are the following: to examine current knowledge about alcohol and its use and abuse; to consider the influences of values, attitudes, and external factors on alcohol use, abuse and addiction; to explore alcohol-related values and help students develop a philosophy regarding personal use of alcohol; to explore the impact of alcohol use and addiction in society; and to help students recognize alcohol-related emergencies and learn appropriate responses (Graham, 1995).

Planning Your Future: Personal and Professional Leadership, offered at the University of Montana, addresses leadership development as it applies to career planning. In this course, students explore their values, goals, and personal and professional leadership development. Each student works with an alumnus or alumna in a career or professional field that matches the student's goals. Students also explore interviewing, résumé writing, and business etiquette to assist them in the transition from the classroom to the real world (Sinz, 1995).

Wake Forest also offers a career development course, Exploration of Career Planning (Taylor, 1995). It examines three specific elements related to career planning: self-assessment, career exploration, and job search strategies.

Learning to Learn is available at Wake Forest and is designed for first- and second-year undergraduates to help them improve their reading and learning skills through the application of basic theory (Chadwick, 1995). It strives to help students improve their vocabulary, reading rate and comprehension, and study skills.

A similar course, Learning Strategies, is taught at IUP to assist students as they learn and apply strategies and principles of self-directedness to college and university life. They learn goal setting and effective time management, develop a study system, and explore the differences between passive and active learning (Ender, 1995b).

Course Materials. A wide variety of materials is used in these courses. About half of the syllabi indicated that textbooks would form the basis of the course's reading material, whereas the other half included required readings such as articles or chapters or provided lists of readings from which students could choose certain selections. The range in the number of readings required, however, was substantial. One course, for example, required twenty-four articles to be read over the course of one quarter. More often, courses with reading lists required at least one reading per week. Other course materials included computer programs such as SIGI-Plus or standardized tests like the Myers-Briggs Type Indicator. Another course required that students purchase a copy of the university calendar of events and an appointment book. Finally, one course used films and videos as course materials.

Instructional Techniques. The teaching techniques used in these courses also varied widely. As this chapter is concerned with the learning process as well as the learning that accrues from this experience, a bit of detail will be provided to describe the learning techniques.

Small-Group Work or Activities. This was very common practice. For example, group techniques were used to get students to work together for a condom-fair project (Willinger, Hansell, and Scholly, 1995). A variation on this approach was used by Dunton (1994), who assigned groups of teams to teach the rest of the class on certain selected topics, such as time management or conflict mediation.

Lecture. Lectures were commonly delivered by the course instructors. Occasionally, guest lecturers presented materials to the students.

Observation. Lowman (1995) points out that many disciplines can benefit from "assignments that ask students to work on projects or make systematic observations outside of class and then integrate their experiences into class discussion or written work" (p. 247). In the case of one course, students were asked to observe a campus or community organization at least two times, and then write a paper describing their observations using specific criteria (team development, meeting management, conflict, communication patterns, and so on) (Johnson and Buford, 1995). Porter, Faulkner, and Wall (1994) have students attend a multicultural event and a multicultural workshop and write a report about their experiences.

Immersion Project. This technique is used by Dunkel (1995). Students select an organization, attend a meeting, and meet with the organization's adviser. They observe the meeting for dynamics, organization, atmosphere and ask the adviser a series of questions. The resulting information forms the basis for an oral class presentation later in the semester and is presented to the instructor in the form of a comprehensive, written report.

Class Presentations. One example of this activity is found in Sinz (1995), where the student is required to make a presentation to the rest of the class on a topic of broad interest to college students. The purpose of the assignment is to help students improve their skills in making persuasive presentations, in addition to providing information to the rest of the class.

Other Active Learning Activities. Another set of learning techniques were employed by Hrabovsky (1995). In this course, one of the goals is to understand the "why of mathematics." Among the techniques used were workshops, computer activities, manipulative activities, and oral and written activities.

Visits. Visits to campus services were listed for several courses. One example is used by Holmes (1994), whose students visit the campus career center and the university advising center to become more familiar with campus services and resources. Ryan and Ladwig (1995) also have students visit the campus library for an orientation tour.

Computer-Assisted Instruction. Although not specifically identified in these courses, computer-assisted instruction has been used successfully in selected classes. Hanjorgiris, DeVito, and Commerford (1993), for example, explain how such instruction is less costly in study skills classes than traditional methods with no dilution in the quality of education.

Evaluation Strategies. A variety of evaluation strategies were employed by those offering the courses identified in this chapter.

Written Papers. A ten- to fifteen-page double-spaced paper was required in Peer Education (Willinger, Hansell, and Scholly, 1995). Students also had to present the paper in class. A five- to seven-page paper based on specific aspects of one book was required for Studies in Contemporary Leadership (Gerardy and Ford, 1995). Students prepare a personal policy paper on "your views of leadership using the concepts covered in the course" for Issues in Leadership (Porteus, Howe, and Jackson, 1995). Writing a paper "stating your observations and assessments in the areas of leadership style, organizational norms and values, group development, team development, meeting management, conflict, and communications patterns" was required of students enrolled in Introduction to Leadership Development (Johnson and Buford, 1995).

Examinations. A final exam administered in class was required for students taking Introduction to Leadership Development (Johnson and Buford, 1995). Ender (1995a) required that students complete a take-home final examination. Two quizzes were part of the evaluation strategy used in Alcohol Studies (Graham, 1995) whereas six quizzes were a part of HHP 395 (Green, 1995).

Journals. Students prepared journal entries in Peer Sexuality (Varley, 1995). Issues in Leadership (Porteus, Howe, and Jackson, 1995) also required students to develop a journal, which should "be a reflective and personal journey that demonstrates an analysis of your leadership from the perspectives represented by each course content area" (p. 2)

Article Reviews. Students reviewed articles and discussed them in class for Advising Student Organizations (Dunkel, 1995) and other courses as well, including Issues in Leadership (Porteus, Howe, and Jackson, 1995).

Class Attendance. Attendance requirements are part of University 100: Academic Success at the University (Henderson, 1995). Planning Your Future required attendance at every class session (Sinz, 1995). More than two absences from this course resulted in a "no pass" grade.

Reaction Papers. Developing a reaction paper synthesizing materials and students' thinking about these materials was required of students in Psychology 101 (Chadwick, 1995). Students completed special projects at the learning assistance office as well as self-modification projects that allowed students to select a problem related to learning that the individual student could solve for himself or herself.

Program Attendance. Attendance at a multicultural event and a multicultural workshop was required of students in Peer Interventions in Diversity Awareness (Porter, Faulkner, and Wall, 1994).

Program Development. Peer Interventions in Diversity Awareness (Porter, Faulkner, and Wall, 1994) required students to create a program module with at least two other people concerning an issue of multiculturalism. An additional module could be created by students for extra credit. Peer Education (Willinger, Hansell, and Scholly, 1995) students prepared a prevention activity relevant to and part of a campus Condom Fair, and a prevention activity as part of National Collegiate Health and Wellness Week.

Interviews. Students interviewed a person they viewed as a leader but whom they did not know well to learn more about styles and experiences other than their own for Issues in Leadership (Porteus, Howe, and Jackson, 1995). A variation on this kind of assignment is employed in Career Development for the College Student (Holleran and Hartzell, 1995), which requires that students interview and shadow a professional of their choice.

Observations and Conclusions

The courses identified in this chapter fit into three categories. First, some of the courses were designed to orient students to college. Whether they were designed for first-time students or returning adults, they attempted to help students feel comfortable with the academic process, learn more about campus resources, and begin to connect with the institution. As Tinto (1987) points out, helping students connect with their institution in an academic and social sense improves retention, which is a general goal of these kinds of courses.

Second, several of these courses attempted to address specific skills that students need. In some cases, the courses addressed academic deficiencies that students often have, while others helped students as they begin to plan their careers and look for employment. In either case, skill development was the general purpose of the course.

The third set of courses provided training for students who either held or sought a position as a paraprofessional on campus. This is a common approach for resident assistants, but it now is being used in other areas such as paraprofessional health advisers, organization advisers, or similar positions.

As mentioned previously, this chapter has not addressed those courses that might be part of the normal curriculum of the institution but happen to be taught by student affairs staff. Among these, for example, might be psychology courses taught by members of the counseling center staff.

Course Materials and Requirements. Fairly standard approaches were taken to providing course materials. Handouts, textbooks, journal articles and so on were commonly used. Nothing particularly innovative or unique was revealed by the analysis of the syllabi used for these courses.

Course requirements were tailored to the learning objectives of the courses. Special projects were required in several courses that very well might not be part of a standard academic course. For example, attendance at a multicultural event was required for the course Interventions in Diversity Awareness (Porter, Faulkner, and Wall, 1994), which also required program development modules on multiculturalism. An immersion project was required for the course designed to help students learn how to advise organizations (Dunkel, 1995), which fits well with the goals of the course.

More often than not, these courses were taught by single instructors, who presumably carried the entire responsibility for delivering the course. Team teaching, assuming that appropriate instructors could be identified and a variety of details were addressed, might be considered for many of these courses. Davis (1995, p. 119) in his study of team teaching concludes that dissatisfaction with team teaching is uncommon and "satisfactions are elaborated with such gusto."

The Future. Will student affairs staff continue to offer courses in the future? It is likely that they will, for several reasons. First, these courses generally have a low cost associated with them. Student affairs staff often teach these courses without receiving a fee for doing so, or if they receive a stipend, it is quite modest. Hence, the instruction is very economical. Second, academic units, at least in some instances, welcome the credit hours produced by these courses. Departments with declining enrollment are pleased to have the credits produced by these courses aggregated in their credit-hour production. Third, the content of these courses is needed. Whether it is offering training courses for paraprofessionals, helping to orient students to college, or pursuing the other objectives identified in this chapter, these courses provide needed content in the curriculum of many institutions. Fourth, student affairs practitioners have the necessary expertise to teach these courses. In fact, in a number of instances they very well may be the campus experts on the topic area and no other member of the faculty or staff would be able to match the skills and knowledge possessed by the student affairs staff. Consequently, they are the logical people to offer the course. Finally, with fewer faculty available on many campuses due to budget reductions, state mandates, or other reasons, student affairs staff offering courses is a method by which instruction can be offered to students without hiring additional faculty or diverting scarce resources from other programs.

As one might surmise, several factors stand in the way of the development of these courses. Three are worthy of comment in this chapter. First, as institutions develop their fee structure so that they charge by the credit hour, having students enroll in the kinds of courses identified in this chapter increases their costs. With the costs to students increasing at an alarming rate, institutions will have to be mindful not to increase costs so that students cannot enroll in these courses. A second issue is that many curricula require that students take more than four years to complete a baccalaureate degree. This is true for many engineering and health professions programs, for example. When students take courses such as those identified in this chapter, they run the risk of prolonging their enrollment or having to take an overload.

Of course, a final issue should not be overlooked. That is, student affairs staff, who normally teach as an overload, may simply not have the energy or time to continue to offer courses. Developing and offering a course is not a simple matter, and as budgets become more stringent and staff are forced to cope with the challenges of contemporary academic life, it is possible that some will opt out of this kind of assignment. There may be an approach or two to help lighten this burden. One is for student affairs staff to team teach courses. This limits the amount of class preparation that each instructor needs to make and the interactive benefits very well could outweigh the extra time required by the teaching assignment. A variation on this would be for a student affairs practitioner to team teach with a member of the regular teaching faculty. Again, the interactive effects may be particularly invigorating and provide a balance for the additional time requirements.

If a student affairs staff member wanted to start a course, but was not sure exactly how to do it, several steps might be considered in planning such an initiative. Certainly a judgment needs to be made as to whether or not the course should be offered. The college (and its students) may not benefit from the course. But if benefits are to be derived from the proposed course, then the person offering it will need to demonstrate mastery of the content area (by holding an appropriate degree and academic experiences) as well as of the appropriate pedagogical techniques. An excellent resource on contemporary teaching techniques has been developed by Menges and Weimar (1996) and could be helpful in this area. The division of student affairs needs to be able to provide the necessary resources for the staff member to offer a course, and this decision has to be made in consultation with the staff member's department head or the senior officer in the division. Finally, a place needs to be found for the course in terms of an academic department, assuming the student affairs division does not have authorization to develop and offer courses. A unit such as education, psychology, sociology, or some similar area is a likely candidate. Often, a unit that can benefit from extra credit-hour production is a good candidate as the academic home. Assuming all these issues can be addressed and resolved, the student affairs staff member can proceed as any faculty member would in developing the course and offering it to students.

The future for student affairs staff to offer courses is bright. Such courses contribute to the vitality of the curriculum, offer needed content, and often provide an exciting way to provide the practical application of concepts from a variety of disciplines. It is likely that more courses of an even greater variety will be taught by student affairs staff in the future.

Syllabi

Chadwick, S. "Learning to Learn" (Psychology 100) (Syllabus). Winston-Salem, N.C.: Wake Forest University, 1995.

Dunkel, N. W. "Advising Student Organizations" (SDS 7930) (Syllabus). Gainesville: University of Florida, 1995.

Dunton, G. "Resident Advising" (EDU 353) (Syllabus). Winston-Salem, N.C.: Wake Forest University, 1994.

Ender, S. C. "Guidance in School Settings" (ED 481) (Syllabus). Indiana, Pa.: Indiana University of Pennsylvania, 1995a.

Ender, S. C. "Learning Strategies" (ED 160) (Syllabus). Indiana, Pa.: Indiana University of Pennsylvania, 1995b.

Gerardy, M., and Ford, M. "Studies in Contemporary Leadership" (ED/HU 358) (Syllabus). Winston-Salem, N.C.: Wake Forest University, 1995.

Graham, C. "Alcohol Studies" (HC 466/566) (Syllabus). Corvallis: Oregon State University, 1995.

Green, L. "HHP 395" (Syllabus). Missoula: University of Montana, 1995.

Henderson, S. H. "University 100: Academic Success at the University" (UNI 100) (Syllabus). Tempe: Arizona State University, 1995.

Holleran, T., and Hartzell, A. "Career Development for the College Student" (No course number provided) (Syllabus). Oneonta, N.Y.: Hartwick College, 1995.

Holmes, T. "General Studies 250: University Seminar" (Syllabus). San Diego: San Diego State University, 1994.

Hrabovsky, P. "Introduction to College Math I" (LC 090) (Syllabus). Indiana, Pa.: Indiana University of Pennsylvania, 1995.

Johnson, N., and Buford, C. "Introduction to Leadership Development" (ED 173) (Syllabus). Santa Barbara: University of California, 1995.

Porter, B., Faulkner, B., and Wall, V. "Peer Interventions in Diversity Awareness" (ECP-400) (Syllabus). Athens, Ga.: University of Georgia, 1994.

Porteus, A., Howe, N., and Jackson, M. "Issues in Leadership" (ED 294-060-095-S-01) (Syllabus). Palo Alto, Calif.: Stanford University, 1995.

Ryan, M., and Ladwig, P. "Returning Adult Seminar" (UC 100A) (Syllabus). Wichita, Kans.: Wichita State University, 1995.

Sinz, J. M. "Planning Your Future: Personal and Professional Leadership" (Honors 395) (Syllabus). Missoula: University of Montana, 1995.

Taylor, B. "Exploration of Career Planning" (Psychology 102) (Syllabus). Winston-Salem, N.C.: Wake Forest University, 1995.

Varley, G. "Peer Sexuality" (ECP 400) (Syllabus). Athens, Ga.: University of Georgia, 1995.

Weldon, F. "Comedy, Creativity and Communication" (C&I 494) (Syllabus). Missoula: University of Montana, 1995.

Willinger, W. M., Hansell, S. M., and Scholly, K. "Contemporary Social/Health Issues and Peer Programming in Higher Education" (EdEP 411[2]) (Syllabus). Manoa: University of Hawaii, 1995.

References

Davis, J. R. *Interdisciplinary Courses and Team Teaching.* Phoenix: American Council on Education and Oryx Press, 1995.

Denson, E. L. "Developing a Freshman Seminar for Athletes." *Journal of College Student Development,* 1994, *35* (4), 303–304.

Dwyer, J. O. "A Historical Look at the Freshman Year Experience." In M. L. Upcraft, J. N. Gardner, and Associates, *The Freshman Year Experience: Helping Students Survive and Succeed in College.* San Francisco: Jossey-Bass, 1989.

Ender, S. C., and Carranza, C. "Students as Paraprofessionals." In T. K. Miller, R. B. Winston, Jr., and Associates, *Administration and Leadership in Student Affairs.* (2nd ed.) Muncie, Ind.: Accelerated Development, 1991.

Ender, S. C., Newton, F. B., and Caple, R. "Student Affairs: Philosophical Models and Program Initiatives, A National Survey of Chief Student Affairs Officers." *A Report to Survey Respondents.* Indiana, Pa.: Indiana University of Pennsylvania, 1996.

Gordon, V. P. "Origins and Purposes of the Freshman Seminar." In M. L. Upcraft, J. N. Gardner, and Associates, *The Freshman Year Experience: Helping Students Survive and Succeed in College.* San Francisco: Jossey-Bass, 1989.

Habley, W. R. "Student Paraprofessionals in Academic Advising." In S. C. Ender and R. B. Winston, Jr. (eds.), *Students as Paraprofessional Staff.* New Directions for Student Services, no. 27. San Francisco: Jossey-Bass, 1984.

Hanjorgiris, W., DeVito, A. J., and Commerford, M. "Computer-Assisted and Classroom Instruction for Study Skills." *Journal of College Student Development,* 1993, *34* (4), 308.

Hardy, D. C., and Karathanos, D. "A Bridge Course for High Risk Freshmen: Evaluating Outcomes." *NASPA Journal,* 1992, *29* (3), 213–221.

Jewler, A. J. "Elements of an Effective Seminar: The University 101 Program." In M. L. Upcraft, J. N. Gardner, and Associates, *The Freshman Year Experience.* San Francisco: Jossey-Bass, 1989.

Lenton, S. M., and Duvall, W. H. "Education of Self." In F. B. Newton and K. L. Ender (eds.), *Student Development Practices.* Springfield, Ill.: Thomas, 1980.

Lowman, J. *Mastering the Techniques of Teaching.* (2nd ed.) San Francisco: Jossey-Bass, 1995.

Menges, R. J., Weimer, M., and Associates. *Teaching on Solid Ground: Using Scholarship to Improve Practice.* San Francisco: Jossey-Bass, 1996.

Robinson, D.A.G. "Career Exploration with Freshman Engineering Students." *Journal of College Student Development,* 1994, *35* (1), 68–69.

Tinto, V. *Leaving College: Rethinking the Causes and Cures of Student Attrition.* Chicago: University of Chicago Press, 1987.

Winston, R. B., Jr., and Fitch, R. T. "Paraprofessional Staffing." In R. B. Winston, Jr., S. Anchors, and Associates, *Student Housing and Residential Life: A Handbook for Professionals Committed to Student Development Goals.* San Francisco: Jossey-Bass, 1993.

JOHN H. SCHUH *is associate vice president for student affairs at Wichita State University, Wichita, Kansas. He has been recognized by the American College Personnel Association and the National Association of Student Personnel Administrators for his contributions to the literature.*

Fundamental shifts in student affairs practices are occurring with student affairs devoting even more time and energy to students' acquisition of knowledge.

Concluding Remarks

Richard B. Caple, Steven C. Ender, Fred B. Newton

We conclude this sourcebook with our thoughts still lingering on the data presented in Chapter One. Our primary purpose through this work has been an assessment and examination of both the reality and potential for our profession's involvement with student learning. We asked chief student affairs officers to give us their opinion on the importance of three philosophical models—service, student development, and learning—that serve as a base for their practice. We also assessed the application of these models through specific questions pertaining to campus programming. At this point, it is important to reflect on what we have learned and offer some thought about how the field of student affairs may be evolving in its contribution to the student learning mission of higher education.

The data presented in Chapter One, although primarily influenced by the student services model, indicates that CSAOs are devoting considerable division time and effort to issues of student development and student learning. We believe this may be explained by a model that includes two sources of order that seem to govern simultaneously the behavior of systems. The first source involves the principle that basic needs dominate the attention and efforts of the organization until such needs are reasonably well satisfied. This principle is Maslowian (Maslow, 1970) in nature. It implies that there are basic levels of need that must be successfully addressed before moving to the next level. General laws govern the adaptive process within a given environment or landscape whether the consideration is biological behavior or economic behavior, for example. Historically, it appears that most if not all student affairs programs began at the level of providing student-oriented services and many in the study (51 percent) reported in Chapter One indicate that this is the source of order that continues to govern their behavior.

But what happens to generate movement from one level to the next? Recent theory indicates that there is a second source of order that functions simultaneously with the first to move a system forward. There is a self-organizing force that can create movement (Caple, 1987a, 1987b; Kauffman, 1993, 1995), which evolves toward a dynamic that is poised between order and chaos and may create a kind of phase transition. Increased complexity within a system can help create a transition to a higher level of functioning. There is no automatic point at which a system will elevate itself to the next level of needs that will dominate its focus, however.

Maslow also theorized that individuals who move to a higher level and subsequently feel the previous level threatened will regress to the more basic level (Maslow, 1968). He indicated that what this meant was a choice between giving up safety or giving up growth. This may parallel organizational growth, too, with programs that have experienced budget cuts and retrenchment demonstrating similar behavior. Self-organizing behavior indicates, however, that once a system moves to a new level it will never be the same again, and although forced to revert to more basic behaviors, it will perform these behaviors, or in the case of student affairs, services, in a different manner than it did before. A recent analysis of corporate growth (Stanley and others, 1996) found that diverse companies followed a somewhat universal growth pattern similar to fundamental laws found in statistical physics. The authors concluded in their analysis of corporate growth that in a system like a college campus, which takes into account many interacting animate subsystems, the important element is the technology of management rather than the technology of production.

No one person in any institution, however, knows the total world of that institution—or the total world of any division or department, for that matter. These systems have all evolved and continue to coevolve within a particular campus landscape. Even when acting intentionally, humans cannot see all the conditions (initial or eventual) that exist for the system they inhabit. These systems are made up of many elements that interact within the boundaries of the system. They may become rigid or frozen, making it difficult to create movement to a new level of behaving, or they may spin out of control and never find a solution for the next level. Each landscape seems to produce its own unique pattern. This is one explanation why no two campuses will take the same approach although there will be clear similarities. Some systems after an additive process of change do coevolve with other systems by finding a transition between the present level of behavior and a new level of order.

Our data do not permit us to do more than suggest the possibility of these constructs. The data represent each respondent at a point in time. There is no way to know how the respondents might have viewed their situation a year before. This survey does provide a baseline for future comparisons, however, and we predict that the future studies will affirm our belief that fundamental shifts in student affairs practices are occurring, with student affairs devoting ever more time and energy to students' acquisition of knowledge. Higher education is about learning. We believe student affairs will continue to reaffirm and strengthen its campus commitment to the learning outcomes of higher education.

References

Caple, R. B. "The Change Process in Developmental Theory: A Self-Organization Paradigm, Part 1." *Journal of College Student Personnel*, 1987a, *28*, 4–11.

Caple, R. B. "The Change Process in Developmental Theory: A Self-Organization Paradigm, Part 2." *Journal of College Student Personnel*, 1987b, *28*, 100–104.

Kauffman, S. A. *The Origins of Order.* New York: Oxford University Press, 1993.

Kauffman, S. *At Home in the Universe.* New York: Oxford University Press, 1995.

Maslow, A. H. *Toward a Psychology of Being.* (2nd ed.) New York: Van Nostrand Reinhold, 1968.

Maslow, A. H. *Motivation and Personality.* (2nd ed.) New York: HarperCollins, 1970.

Stanley, M.H.R., Amaral, L.A.N., Buldyrev, S. V., Shlomo, H., Heiko, L., Maass, P., Salinger, M. A., and Stanley, H. E. "Scaling Behaviour in the Growth of Companies." *Nature*, 1996, *379* (29), 804–806.

RICHARD B. CAPLE *is director of counseling and professor of education at the University of Missouri–Columbia.*

STEVEN C. ENDER *is professor in the Learning Center, Division of Student Affairs, at Indiana University of Pennsylvania.*

FRED B. NEWTON *is director of counseling and professor of counseling and educational psychology at Kansas State University.*

RESOURCES

This section provides a list of colleges and universities whose programs, courses, and campus interventions are shared in this sourcebook. Readers are encouraged to contact these institutions if additional information is desired.

Chapter Two

Akron University, Counseling, Testing & Career Center, 163 Simmons Hall, Akron OH 44325–4303

California State University at Fullerton, P.O. Box 34060, Fullerton CA 92634–9460

Centralia College, 600 West Locust, Centralia WA 98531

Colorado State University, Housing and Food Services—Palmer Center, Fort Collins CO 80523–0002

Eastern Montana College, 1500 N. 30th Street, Billings MT 59101

Gallaudet University, Northwest Campus, 1640 Kalmia Road NW, Washington DC 20012

Kansas State University, Housing & Dining Services, Pittman Building, Manhattan KS 66506

Kansas State University, Academic Assistance Center, Holton Hall, Manhattan KS 66506

Kansas State University, University Counseling Services, Lafene Health Center, Manhattan KS 66506

LaGuardia Community College, 31–10 Thomson Avenue, Long Island City NY 11101

Michigan State University, W-185 Holmes Hall, East Lansing MI 48825

North Seattle Community College, 9600 College Way North, Seattle WA 98103

Notre Dame College of Ohio, South Euclid OH 44121–4293

Southwest Texas State University, 601 University Drive, San Marcos TX 78666

Stanford University, 765 Pampas Lane, Stanford CA 94305–7210

Texas Tech University, Counseling Center, P.O. Box 45008, Lubbock TX 79409

Thiel College, 75 College Avenue, Greenville PA 16125

University of Illinois at Urbana–Champaign, Counseling Center, 212 Student Services Bldg., Champaign IL 61820

University of Kentucky, 218 Service Bldg., Lexington KY 40506

University of Louisville, Counseling Center, Louisville KY 40292

University of Maryland at College Park, 2101 Annapolis Hall, College Park MD 20742

University of Missouri–Rolla, Counseling & Career Development, Rolla MO 65401

University of Nebraska–Lincoln, 1100 Seaton Hall, Lincoln NE 68588–0622
University of New Mexico, 201 La Posada Hall, Albuquerque NM 87131
University of Washington, Housing & Food Services, Box 355842, Seattle WA 98195–5842
University of Waterloo, Counseling Services, NH 2080, Waterloo, Ontario, CANADA N2L 3G1
University of Wisconsin–Oshkosh, 800 Algoma Blvd., Oshkosh WI 54901
Valparaiso University, Student Counseling & Development Center, Valparaiso IN 46383
Walla Walla Community College, 500 Tausick Way, Walla Walla WA 99362
Worcester Polytechnic Institute, 100 Institute Road, Worcester MA 01609
Yale University, 155 Whitney Avenue, New Haven CT 06511

Chapter Five

Bethel College, Box 280, McKenzie TN 38201
Illinois State University, Campus Box 2700, Normal IL 61790–2700
Transylvania University, 300 North Broadway, Lexington KY 40508–1797
Tusculum College, Greeneville TN 37743–9997
University of Alaska, 3211 Providence Drive BEB 106, Anchorage AK 99518
University of Evansville, 1800 Lincoln Avenue, Evansville IN 47722
University of Idaho, Student Counseling Center, Moscow ID 83844–1099
University of Missouri–Rolla, 204 Norwood Hall, Rolla MO 65401–0249
University of South Carolina, Columbia SC 29208
West Virginia University, Box 6009, Morgantown WV 26506–6009

Chapter Six

Carson-Newman College, P.O. Box 71892, Jefferson City TN 37760
Indiana University, 801 North Jordan Avenue, Bloomington IN 47405
Michigan State University, East Lansing MI 48825
University of California–Davis, First & A Street, Davis CA 95616–8712
University of Central Arkansas, UCA P.O. Box 4937, Conway AR 72032
University of Louisville, Housing and Residence Life, Louisville KY 40292
University of Miami, 1211 Dickinson Drive, Coral Gables FL 33146
University of Michigan–Ann Arbor, 515 East Jefferson Street, Ann Arbor MI 48109–1316
University of Missouri–St Louis, 8001 Natural Bridge Road, St Louis MO 63121
University of Nevada-Las Vegas, Box 452013, 4505 South Maryland Parkway, Las Vegas NV 89154–2013
University of Pittsburgh at Johnstown, Johnstown PA 15904
University of Washington, Box 353760, Seattle WA 98195–3760
University of Wisconsin–Madison, 625 Babock Drive, Madison WI 53706
Western Illinois University, 1 University Circle, Macomb IL 61455

INDEX

Ordering Information

NEW DIRECTIONS FOR STUDENT SERVICES is a series of paperback books that offers guidelines and programs for aiding students in their total development—emotional, social, and physical, as well as intellectual. Books in the series are published quarterly in Spring, Summer, Fall, and Winter and are available for purchase by subscription as well as individually.

SUBSCRIPTIONS cost $52.00 for individuals (a savings of 35 percent over single-copy prices) and $79.00 for institutions, agencies, and libraries. Standing orders are accepted. New York residents, add local sales tax for subscriptions. (For subscriptions outside the United States, add $7.00 for shipping via surface mail or $25.00 for air mail. Orders *must be prepaid* in U.S. dollars by check drawn on a U.S. bank or charged to VISA, MasterCard, or American Express.)

SINGLE COPIES cost $20.00 plus shipping (see below) when payment accompanies order. California, New Jersey, New York, and Washington, D.C., residents, please include appropriate sales tax. Canadian residents, add GST and any local taxes. Billed orders will be charged shipping and handling. No billed shipments to post office boxes. (Orders from outside the United States *must be prepaid* by check drawn on a U.S. bank or charged to VISA, MasterCard, or American Express.)

SHIPPING (SINGLE COPIES ONLY): one issue, add $5.00; two issues, add $6.00; three issues, add $7.00; four to five issues, add $8.00; six to seven issues, add $9.00; eight or more issues, add $12.00.

ALL PRICES are subject to change.

DISCOUNTS FOR QUANTITY ORDERS are available. Please write to the address below for information.

ALL ORDERS must include either the name of an individual or an official purchase order number. Please submit your order as follows:
   Subscriptions: specify series and year subscription is to begin
   Single copies: include individual title code (such as SS55)

MAIL ALL ORDERS TO:
   Jossey-Bass Publishers
   350 Sansome Street
   San Francisco, California 94104-1342

FOR SUBSCRIPTION SALES OUTSIDE OF THE UNITED STATES, contact any international subscription agency or Jossey-Bass directly.